How to Make Your Car LAST A LIFETIME

Bob Fendell

Holt,
Rinehart
and Winston

New York

Published by Holt, Rinehart and Winston,
383 Madison Avenue, New York, New York 10017.

Published simultaneously in Canada by
Holt, Rinehart and Winston of Canada, Limited.

Library of Congress Cataloging in Publication Data

Fendell, Bob, 1925–
How to make your car last a lifetime.
Includes index.
1. Automobiles—Maintenance and repair. I. Title.
TL152.F38   629.28′722   80–19759
ISBN Hardcover: 0–03–053661–8
ISBN Paperback: 0–03–053656–1
First Edition
Designer: Lana Giganti
Printed in the United States of America
10 9 8 7 6 5 4 3 2 1

Acknowledgments

This book would not
have been possible
without the cooperation
of all levels of the auto
industry, witting and
unwitting, the efforts of
the likes of Ed Mullane
and Betty Levy, and the
understanding of my
wife, Elaine.

Contents

Preface

Barring accident or the Apocalypse, there is no recent American automobile that will not last at least 150,000 miles, and some may be capable of lasting double that distance.

We believe this because, despite any bad experiences you may have had, the car makers themselves expect their products to last for ten years and for at least 100,000 miles, given recommended maintenance. What is more, they have been increasingly eager to do something about the shortcomings in their products that surface when in public use rather than in the company testing environment. It's not because they want to build you a vehicle that lasts forever; it's because of Uncle Sam and the awesome expense of recalling anywhere up to 16 million vehicles and paying for repair of the flaw out of their own pocket. The law mandating recall campaigns has done more to propel Detroit and the imports toward zero defect vehicles than all the industry critics put together. And that means you have a better chance at making the car last and last.

If you take the extra precautions and follow the procedures suggested in this book, you can achieve mileage and durability beyond your present dreams. And this despite road salt in the North, potholes and deteriorating secondary roads, sticky fingers, cigarette ash, and engines that run hotter and harder as the industry acquires and gradually applies the knowhow to ensure less pollution and more gas mileage.

But why should anyone raised in the American way of dynamic obsolescence even think of making his present or next car last a lifetime? Why indeed!

The primary reason is to save enough money to maintain your freedom of transportation. Consider these facts:

- The average cost of a new U.S. automobile has risen in just three years from $4,800 to $6,800. That's $2,000 —or about 42 percent.

- There is no chance that general list prices on automobiles will fall. In truth, some auto analysts project a minimum 4.5 percent rise in each of the next three years. That would turn your $4,800 average car into a $7,500 average car in a six-year span.

- A Chevrolet Impala, most popular *full-sized* automobile in America, cost $3,400 in 1973. There now is no American or foreign-built *subcompact* that costs that little.

- Used-car prices have risen at a similar pace, although it is more difficult to generalize about their cost increase.

This rising cost of automobile acquisition is what makes the idea of coping by keeping so attractive. But there's more. Consider these facts, too:

- In 1974 after the first oil crisis, a gallon of gasoline cost 49¢ many places. In just two months of 1979—May and June—gas prices rose some 20¢ to 25¢ to break the $1-a-gallon price barrier in the same locales. What is the price of gas now where you are?

- The price of auto insurance in the *best* areas doubled in four years. This is deceptively low; for some categories of people and some vehicles, the rise was fourfold or more.

- And the mechanics' labor rates for repair and other service at car dealerships has more than doubled in most parts of the United States in three years.

If all these statistics are discouraging, think about something encouraging. When you try to make your car last longer, you will not be alone. New-car buyers already are waiting some 4.4 years before trading, instead of 2.5 years as late as 1976. So obviously American cars *can* last longer and still be useful and attractive.

Of course, there may be other factors contributing to this stretchout—like installment contracts made over such a long period that often the buyer doesn't own the car until after four years; or people who would rather eat and keep warm than have a shiny new car.

If you think about it, you may have other more subjective reasons for wanting to make a particular vehicle last —matters of taste, thoughts of profitable investment by collecting, or other reasons. The key question is, What does keeping the car entail? That is also what this book is about.

If you get the idea that we believe it well-nigh impossible to make a car last and last without some investment of your own elbow grease, you are 100 percent correct. But it's worth it—the sense of accomplishment that pervades a seven-thumbed nonmechanical person when he saves the time, effort, and money of going to the nearest garage is one of the few nonsexual satisfactions in life that anyone can attain.

Cerebral types and most people under forty from white-collar homes believe they have been forbidden to get their hands dirty from a car. Yet these same people think nothing of rooting around in a garden or doing myriad other activities calculated to create a mixture of sweat and grime that no self-respecting automobile mechanic would countenance. If you abhor dirt or grease under your fingernails, plastic gloves are available at the local supermarket.

Thus, you can find out safely that hands are made for something else besides holding cigarettes or pressing the button on the automatic TV-channel switcher. It is a matter of mind over matter. If intellectually you can perceive the benefits of the permanent car—even if this perception is aided by so crass a consideration as need—then you must concede it would be illogical not to gain these benefits in the most expeditious and economical manner possible. What you know means nothing unless you put that knowledge to

work by trusting your own ability, ingenuity, and persever-
ance.

There is another benefit in self-reliance. You do not need
to waste time getting the vehicle to the garage at the
convenience of the garage. An oil change may take ten
minutes, five of them waiting for the oil to drain out fully.
Are you going to take the time to drive back and forth to the
garage to save the possibility of the minor physical exercise
an oil change entails? The correct answer is no, no, a
thousand times no.

This book isn't anti–new car or anti–anything else. It is
pro-you. If you are prepared to take the actions necessary; if
you are prepared to think of the automobile as something
that can be made continually desirable and kept that way; if
you are prepared to save money and aggravation—read on.

Bob Fendell

How to Make
Your Car
Last a LIFETIME

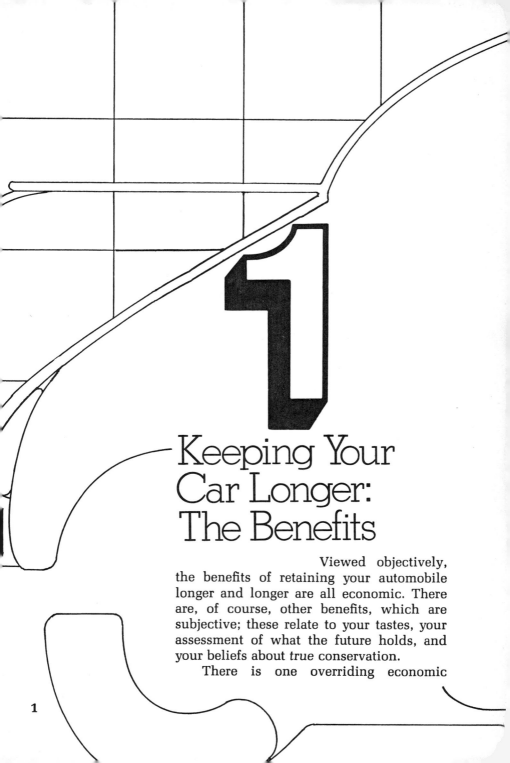

Keeping Your Car Longer: The Benefits

Viewed objectively, the benefits of retaining your automobile longer and longer are all economic. There are, of course, other benefits, which are subjective; these relate to your tastes, your assessment of what the future holds, and your beliefs about *true* conservation.

There is one overriding economic

1

benefit. By keeping your car longer, you remove yourself from the installment-credit cycle. A $6,000 loan for 48 months at a 13 percent true annual rate of interest—a low percentage at this writing—costs you $1,726 extra (28.75 percent of the original loan), not counting the credit life and credit disability insurance that the bank or dealership will most likely try to sell you. (You must consider true annual percentage rates, not monthly payments, if you are to be aware of the money installment credit is costing. The monthly payment on that loan would be about $161 plus the insurance extras; that tells you nothing about the full cost.)

If you don't buy, that $1,726 is in your pocket, not the bank's. More important, if you don't buy, you don't need to make the $6,000 loan in the first place, so the real saving from skipping one trade-in cycle is $7,726 for the case postulated. And we didn't figure the amount you spend in barter when you trade your present car as a down payment.

By skipping a trade-in cycle, you are taking yourself out of the depreciation game—the more so the longer you keep your present car. Let us compare a man who traded after four years and one who waited. Assuming identical cars in identical condition at the same time of year in the same market area, the nontrader saves the 80 percent depreciation. In fact, to the nontrader these factors don't make any difference. How can we say this?

Read slowly, because this may be tricky for some people. Both cars depreciated 80 percent on paper, but the person trading makes that paper figure an irrevocable fact. In contrast, the nontrader really doesn't care about the paper figure, even though he may be writing off the depreciation on his income tax. He never loses the depreciation unless and until the vehicle is sold, it leaves his possession in some other way, or it becomes permanently inoperable. If that happens, say sixteen years hence, the value of the average car long since has been depreciated out and his depreciation loss per year over the life of the vehicle is one-quarter that of the first man—or less.

The Internal Revenue Service has been allowing vehicles to be totally depreciated out for tax purposes in five years, either at the straight-line rate of 20 percent per year or by a graduating scale that cuts the value of the car some 40 percent the first year and lesser percentages after that. After five years the residual value will vary with the individual automobile.

In some cases the residual value itself is an economic reason for keeping a car longer when the model is no longer available. This depends on your assessment of the future. There are people—we have no idea how many—who bought Cadillac convertibles in 1978 for investment purposes. These were the last Cadillac convertibles, there were a limited number, and therefore these people reasoned that if they kept the vehicle for a decade or so they would have a collector's item that would be worth more then than now. Many of these vehicles were put into storage and will be in close to new condition when the owner decides the time is ripe to test the market.

Dazzled by the incredible prices good antique or classic vehicles bring (a 1959 Thunderbird may bring more than its original list price), a whole host of people regard cars as collectibles. It is a hobby and, since most drive the vehicles rather than store them, it is also transportation.

Right now we are witnessing the demise of entire size categories and car models; whole engine-displacement classes are disappearing, too. There is plenty of grist for collectors. What the collector must determine is whether anyone else will want the cars he preserves enough to pay a premium price. We make only one point. It's easier to realize you have a classic after five years than to go out and try to spot one the first model year out. And it's usually more profitable.

In considering how long to retain your vehicle, there are two key phrases. We just used one—residual value. The other is not quite the same—useful life. *Residual value* after the first five years depends upon the make of car, the particular model, the year, the vehicle's condition, and maybe even equipment and color. *Useful life* depends merely upon whether the vehicle will run or not and whether it will do the job it needs to do for you. A 1955 Chevrolet V-8 coupe has more residual value than a 1961 Chevrolet sedan because some consider it a classic. The 1961, however, may have a longer useful life if it is in better shape.

If you retain your vehicle longer and longer, your primary consideration shifts from its residual value to its useful life. Once you make this mental adjustment, you look at your vehicle from a different perspective. In essence, you are saying to yourself, "What can I do to keep this car trouble-free longer?" instead of "How can I keep this car so it will look as good as possible when I trade it in?"

That adjustment in itself may be of more than economic benefit, because it means you are moving from preserving the appearance to preserving the unseen items, too. One other thing to remember: you have little control over a vehicle's residual value; you have almost total control over its useful life.

However, another economic "benefit" for those who have older models is, we believe, overrated and perhaps transient—the ability to run on leaded or "regular" gasoline. Yes, there is a price differential between leaded and unleaded gasoline. Assume your older vehicle gets a national-average 14 mpg (miles per gallon) and you drive 10,000 miles a year; you are then using about 714 gallons of gas annually. If the price differential is 5¢ a gallon, you save $35.70 a year, or some $357 over a decade.

The benefit disappears quickly if you move from a 14-mpg vehicle to a more modern one rated at 21 mpg. It also disappears if the lead in the gas increases maintenance costs: in particular, upkeep on spark plugs. It only holds if you succeed in bringing the vehicle closer to 21 mpg. This can be done at a price substantially less than the cost of a new car. On some cars better tires give a quick 2 to 3 mpg more; a replacement carburetor that rids you of excess power can add up to 3 mpg or more. And there are other things you can do which we discuss in later chapters.

What if a car fits your taste, life style, and need for space, and you have it running as efficiently as possible? Why change? If that satisfactory car is of a size no longer on the market, we believe it is illogical to get rid of it—given the fact that the alternative of buying two or more vehicles to replace one is not a possible choice for many. Why should you face double insurance and double maintenance bills, and have a situation that is not only less to your liking but sociologically wasteful, too? If a 35-mpg vehicle carries two people and a 17.5-mpg vehicle carries four, aren't they equally transportation-efficient?

There is a further benefit to keeping a car we know to be true but, because no market researcher or psychologist has made a formal study, we cannot refer you to statistics.

Most will admit that driving a car is a continuous learning experience. We believe one of the things you learn is the automobile itself. Its characteristics become familiar to you and you feel safer and probably more comfortable driving it. It may not in fact be either safe or comfortable: that is your perception, and of course you should consider squaring reality with your perception. But your confidence with this car helps it become part of your ways—you know how it handles, starts, stops, and you want its successor to be equally familiar.

The car manufacturers know this, and that is why they are jittery and perhaps confused. General Motors thought long and hard before moving front-wheel drive from a luxury vehicle to its mass-market compacts. Why? Because front-wheel drive by its nature steers differently and feels different. General Motors was willing to sacrifice that difference to make the new compact front-wheel-drive cars feel and steer as nearly like the conventional rear-drive layout as possible. Thus the customer does not feel the oversteer inherent in front-wheel drive. (Oversteer is the tendency of the car to try to straighten a curve.) *Correction: Understeer*

Obviously, if you keep the same car you are driving, you won't have any such problems. But in that case you must guard against too much familiarity. Your body gets used to bad shock absorbers, for instance, and will compensate for gradual deterioration of safety-related items.

Finally, we believe you can feel very righteous and patriotic about keeping your present car longer and longer. In a world of finite resources, you are using the energy and materials consumed in its manufacture more efficiently each year you keep it.

When any manufactured product is scrapped, so is the energy consumed in making it and transporting it to market. The new product replacing it also requires the energy of manufacture and transport, most likely at a higher current dollar rate, if we are to believe the auto industry's justification for continuously higher retail prices.

Thus *you* are the true conservator, assuming always that the product is useful to you and continues to do its job.

Our point is not that nothing should ever be consigned to the scrap heap; it is that *new* is not better by definition nor is *old* or *used* undesirable or less useful. A new car may or may not afford certain benefits of mechanics, comfort, or appearance. The prospective buyer must weigh the benefits he perceives against the savings and benefits of his present vehicle. This is a case-by-case choice.

We might note, however, that the automobile is changing so rapidly these days in real ways—not just changes in the grille or the styling—that, for the next several years at least, it may be better to retain a vehicle with which you are familiar if it is still capable of giving you good service. Other people have said it many times: when something really new comes out, let the other fellow be the pioneer.

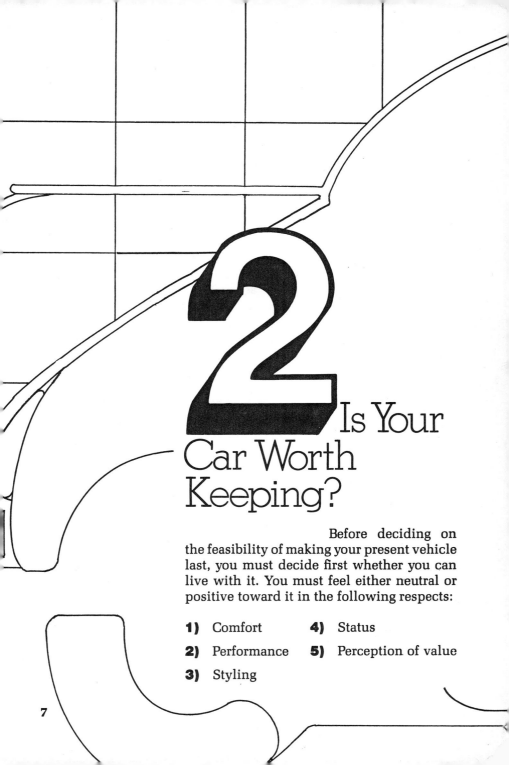

2 Is Your Car Worth Keeping?

Before deciding on the feasibility of making your present vehicle last, you must decide first whether you can live with it. You must feel either neutral or positive toward it in the following respects:

1) Comfort　　　**4)** Status

2) Performance　**5)** Perception of value

3) Styling

Comfort **|** There is no way you'll keep a car long if you think you don't fit or if your knee bangs the console or if some factor like seating annoys and frustrates you.

Of course, in some cases, the defect can be eliminated —as in the case of the seats—but mostly these factors will be basic irretrievable defects of design. If so, forget about the car as a means of daily transport.

Performance **|** Performance is another matter. If all or most other factors are favorable, the performance of any car can be improved. There is a large cadre of vehicles out in the real world with engines that are marginal for their weight. Car companies spewed them out—they still do—more to meet the government's mandates for corporate average fuel economy than to provide balanced transport for the people buying them.

And while these vehicles may perform EPA certification-testing and gas-mileage cycles in great style, in the real world they may be less gas-efficient than the next larger engine.

The ultimate way to improve performance is to replace the engine. A less-expensive alternative available for some cars is to change or alter the carburetor or even to switch to fuel injection. Others we discuss later.

Styling **|** Styling is an equally easy factor to alter. But since this is such a subjective matter, you must decide if you can make a particular car acceptable by removing or altering trim, by stripping, or by changing the color. If major exterior changes are necessary, you usually won't be happy with paint jobs and trim.

Styling is inside, too. Think about new carpet, seat covers, new door panels. Will any one or a combination make the car acceptable? Perhaps just a thorough cleaning and protective coating would do the job.

Status | Status is another intangible. There are a number of automobile nameplates that convey status to many people. There are other cases where a model designation—like RX-7, Monte Carlo, Seville, T-Bird—means instant status. And still other people groove on the way the car is equipped. These taste differences are what has made the automobile industry an incredible business.

Status is so subjective that a white Seville would be all right, but if you drive up to the club in a rose-colored one you're apt to be ostracized or at least gossiped about. Yet the rose car may be done artistically.

Perception of Value | Your friends' perceptions of what is status really colors your decision even if you won't admit it. And that in turn colors your perception of the automobile's value. Logically, the vehicle may never have given you trouble, may be comfortable, and may even be exciting transportation, but if it elicits negative comment from friends, your perception of its value will drop.

If you are the rare rugged individual you'll shrug this off. But there are very few rugged individuals. If you are not convinced that your candidate for permanent automobile represents good value over the years, look for something else. That is why starting with a new or nearly new car is so good; people rarely look down on new cars and less is likely to be wrong.

For the great majority of us, however, there already is a car in our life and we either would rather not or couldn't consider buying a new one at this point in time. And if you are one of a not insignificant number of people who have examined new cars and found Old Faithful looking better and better, then you need to assess the factors in getting the vehicle into condition to go for the long pull.

Does that mean it must gleam in the sunlight like a commercial for car polish? No, it doesn't. It means it must be able to do its job—and that means getting it looking great must take a back seat to getting it working and running great.

What you cannot and must not neglect is anything associated with safety or mobility. Examples of safety-related items are tires and wheels and window glass. An example of mobility is the condition of any part of the engine or transmission. If your 80,000-mile Plymouth passes muster in that respect, then we believe you can begin to consider it as a candidate to keep.

Certainly, it is difficult for an American to drive a vehicle coruscated by rust and having an interior of less than living-room quality. We are told from the moment we become aware of automobiles that "shiny" is desirable and denotes newness. Actually at the 55-mph (miles per hour) speeds we are supposed to be traveling, a slippery shiny outer surface of itself makes almost no real difference in speed or efficiency. Unless you are as unusual or creative as the furrier who some years ago clad an entire car in fake mink, however, your forever car likely will be as shiny and sleek as you can keep it.

Let's restate the key question. How do you make the judgment to spend money to ensure maximum life for the car? What should be obvious, we reiterate, is that even major repairs are less expensive than buying a new car. However, as you estimate costs, you need to factor in the downtime to get the repairs done (when you'll need other means of transport) and you need to assess what you will have after you have made the changes. Remember also that you are doing all this to save money, so, after buying safety items, decide how little of the rest you can live with. Let's go into more detail.

Bumpers | Unless you have a vehicle with a so-called soft fascia, the bumper is likely to be chromed steel. In usage without protection, the chrome wears and eventually rust appears. You also pick up dents and dimples and the tips sometimes get bent. If looks are important, there's nothing more important to renewing a vehicle than getting the bumpers straightened and rechromed. However, the bumpers work just as well with worn spots. If you rechrome bumpers, rechrome everything else at the same time; we are told it will cost relatively less.

Body | Check that the hood, the trunk lid, and the doors fit properly. Get them realigned—especially the doors, which must not squeak during opening and closing. If they won't stay aligned, then you may have a misaligned frame.

Check the paint job for dents and scratches. Are there many nicks along the edges of the doors, hood, and trunk lid? Check for bubbly spots, which are signs of emerging rust, and rust-through, where the metal is totally eaten away. Rust is an especially serious problem in the frame members or, in unit-body vehicles, the load-bearing areas. You can patch some rusted-through spots but not all. You should check the seriousness of the bubbly spots, which most often occur around the rear window, near the wheel wells, and on some cars under headlights and taillights and on the rear door sill. Get an estimate of what it will cost to repaint and straighten dents and patch rust. Stay with the color the car is now unless you absolutely can't stand it.

Another option, if you have a relatively popular car, is to check the local junkyard for body parts from a wreck. It sometimes is better and cheaper to replace rusted or badly dented fenders, quarter panels, hoods, and trunk lids that way.

Suspension | The suspension includes the shock absorbers, the springs or torsion bars, and the attachments thereof, including bushings. It is highly unlikely you are riding around with a broken spring, but very likely you may need new shocks. Do the bounce test: press both hands on the edge of each fender as far forward as possible and as hard as you can. The corner of the car should not go up and down more than once. Otherwise you may need shock absorbers. That's something

you should get right away for safety's sake. Get premium
shocks if you can—the ride may improve so much you will
have your mind made up for you.

Alignment | Go to a deserted level large parking lot. Get up to

about 15 to 20 mph. Loosen your grip on the steering wheel
for a short time, letting up on the accelerator. Does the car
wander to left or right? If it does, it means either your wheels
are not aligned or a brake is grabbing. In either case, the
problem affects your safety, and you should make the repair
whether or not you expect to keep the car for a long time.

Under the Hood | If your car starts easily, runs smoothly, and

doesn't overheat or stall, you must believe there is nothing
major wrong with it. Now, with the motor off, take a look.
Even if you can't tell a radiator from a carburetor, you still
can look and feel under the hood. Just be careful. Never
smoke. Also, it's safer to make your examination when the
car has been idle for some time.

You know what hoses are. Do they look cracked or
frayed? Feel them. Are they stiff and do the attachment
points have whitish stains? One end goes into something in
front; that's the radiator. Does it have stains on it? Are the
fins bent or damaged?

The other end goes into the engine block, which also has
wires going out of it and usually one or two things that look
like oversized ice trays on or near the top. Are the wires
cracked or frayed? Is there wet oil anywhere on the block? Or
is the oily dirt especially thick? Any affirmatives mean a trip
to your local repairman.

There are other components under the hood. Just check
to make sure everything is attached to something. If it's very
dirty under there, you can either clean off the engine with
special cleaner or pay for a steam cleaning. Either way you
are then in a position to monitor how quickly the oily dirt
comes back and whether the wires and hoses deteriorate
rapidly.

Obviously if the car doesn't run well, you know that there will be repairs. Just note in your own mind and words what is unacceptable; then write it down and go off to the repairman.

Wheels ❘ Check first the amount of tread left on the tires. Do the
Lincoln-penny test. Insert a penny into tread, Lincoln's nose facing out. If his beard shows, tire replacement is due. It is due—and you may have alignment or brake problems—if you find flat spots or very uneven wear.

If there are any wheel covers, take them off. Check for dark stains around the hub or on the wheel itself. You may have a leaky brake system if the stains are pronounced. Another item you should check is where the wheel grips the tire. If this edge is bent or any part of it stands away from the tire, you may have a damaged wheel. So there are a few more possible expenses.

Interior ❘ You can see pretty quickly the condition of the seats,
carpeting, and trim. Seat covers will mask seat blemishes, but not a broken seat spring or a seat that has sagged from use. Does the carpeting need replacement? What is the condition of the door trim and dashboard? Are any knobs or covers or door handles missing? Are seat belts in good condition? Probably—and unfortunately—they're less worn than the rest of the interior. The very least you should do is clean the interior thoroughly before making judgments. Do the trunk, too, if there is one.

Windows, Mirrors, and Lights ❘ Clean the windows and mir-
rors. You can see large damage easily, but then examine for tiny scratches in window glass, particularly the windshield. They heighten glare and make it harder to see. Check mirrors for reflective value, ability to adjust. Check lights and lenses. In some states, your headlights must be aligned and working.

We see it all the time, but we cannot understand people who drive with one headlight or taillight out of commission.

We didn't cover every item—the exhaust system, for instance—but you should. When you have completed this detailed survey of your vehicle, you may be shocked by the cost of getting it into top shape, especially if you have neglected to maintain it properly. If so, consider doing the refurbishing job on the "installment" plan—safety first, comfort second, and cosmetics last.

You *can* replace the engine or the transmission or major components of the suspension or body and still be ahead of the game. Really what it comes down to is determining what is good on the vehicle, starting from the inside out.

If you have owned the car since it was new, you can answer certain key questions.

> Has it been in an accident that crushed the front end to the point where the vehicle needed to be towed on a hook?

> Has it been in any other accident that twisted the chassis to the point where it needed straightening? Such an accident may have bashed in a rear fender, severely bent the door or quarter panel, or destroyed a wheel *and* suspension or steering components.

If the answer to either question is yes, we personally would hesitate to keep this vehicle unless there was some overriding reason—not because it may not have been repaired properly but because we now are talking about forever. When metal is stretched or re-formed, there is an element of stress placed upon it. Unless you wish to magna-flux the chassis (subject it to molecular examination via a special machine) and other repaired members of the suspension or steering, discretion says you pass on this car.

It may last ten years or forever, but then again, what happens if you have another less serious accident? It may be enough to throw the chassis out of alignment again. The result will be doors that don't fit and parts that creak and even—in extreme cases—a car that can never be aligned properly.

What else should disqualify a car or truck?

Don't keep it if the frame—or, in unit-body vehicles, a large load-bearing area—is rusted through. By this we mean eaten away so that the stress area can collapse, not just surface discoloration. This can happen easily with a flood- or salt-damaged vehicle that some unscrupulous rat sold as new. You can sometimes check if a car or truck is water-damaged by lifting the carpet (which may have been re-placed) to examine the underlayment or even lifting the underlayment to check for whitish stains on the floor. Also check the side liners under the dash for white or for signs of repainting.

If you still feel you have no way to judge whether yours is a vehicle to be made to last, go to an authority figure such as the man who has been repairing your vehicle. *Don't* ask him if he thinks you can make the vehicle last forever. Ask him what the brand's idiosyncrasies are, including rust problems, the repair record, or front-end problems.

For relatively recent automobiles, you can use maga-zines as an authority. *Consumer Reports* publishes a frequency-of-repair index; if nothing else, it gives you another opinion. *Popular Mechanics* and *Road & Track* both run reports based upon extended use, the former from owners and the latter from its experts.

Don't decide only on such evidence. Your vehicle may be better or worse than the vehicles described in generalized comments. If you own a Pinto with a handling package, radial tires, custom interior, and a premium sound system, it is likely to be a better candidate than one without those items.

Whether or not you can live with such basic point-to-point transportation as the Pinto is your choice. It has to its advantage relative simplicity and to its disadvantage the cheapest everything. There's surely plenty to change and upgrade, and one model of the Pinto—the Pony—could be purchased for well under $4,000 new. But a Pinto advocate would have done much better to choose the well-equipped $4,500 version and have gotten better interior, better tires, and a better base for long usage. The same would apply to most economy and low-end cars.

Thus, you must inspect the vehicle and evaluate other factors to learn the value—to you—of retaining your car. Just add up the cost factors and the personal factors. You'll know if it's a "go."

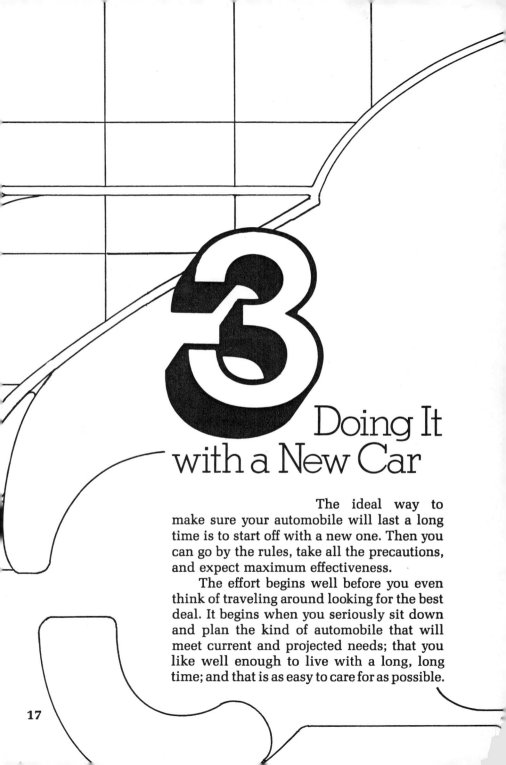

3 Doing It with a New Car

The ideal way to make sure your automobile will last a long time is to start off with a new one. Then you can go by the rules, take all the precautions, and expect maximum effectiveness.

The effort begins well before you even think of traveling around looking for the best deal. It begins when you seriously sit down and plan the kind of automobile that will meet current and projected needs; that you like well enough to live with a long, long time; and that is as easy to care for as possible.

Meeting Your Needs | The primary function of an automobile is

to transport you and whomever and whatever you wish to transport, whenever you wish to take them, to wherever you can get. Your primary car may be your later-life substitute for thumb-sucking, it may be more fun than making wood furniture, and it may be many other things; but if it doesn't transport you adequately, it's a failure.

Now, if you are affluent enough to maintain two or three vehicles, you may assign different functions to each. In that case, you must decide which function this new vehicle will fulfill. If it is going to be a toy, then we assume that your attention span has grown since the days when you fished the Buck Rogers Zap Gun out from under the Christmas tree, zapped all the people on your personal hit list, and then immediately relegated it to the corner of the toy chest next to the Hans Brinker attachable skate blades. You want this toy to last and continue to give you pleasure.

How do you know what your needs are? More importantly, how can you project your needs into the future? The following questions will suggest how you can think this through. You may think it through differently, but the important thing is to think and reason before you buy, to avoid being disappointed or even enraged after you buy thoughtlessly.

How many people do you want it to carry most of the time? Will this change in the next six or seven years?

How much cargo—suitcases, grocery bags, fertilizer, plywood panels—do you usually carry? Remember passengers, too, and if you are likely to ask it to be a tow car, consider that.

What kind of service will it be in? Mostly around town or in the suburbs, mostly over the highway for long trips, mostly on secondary or twisty rural or mountain roads, or mostly for commuting to a big city? Will this change in the years ahead?

Do you expect to work on the car yourself for most repairs and maintenance, or will it be maintained by a mechanic?

Obviously, if you belong to a two-person family and a baby is either planned or on the way, you'll need more than two seats. If you are part of an extended family and will have relatives in the car all the time, you need to think of a five- or six-passenger vehicle. Conversely, if your offspring are moving into their own automobiles or have flown the coop, you can consider smaller, sportier, and more economical transport.

In the matter of cargo, if you are past the stage of bringing home bags of fertilizer or plywood sheets or if you never reached that stage and don't intend to, you don't need a large station wagon. If you fly to vacations, a small car will suffice to get the suitcases to the airport and back. If the only time you tow or pack a great deal of cargo is once or twice a year, wouldn't it be more economical to rent a car for those few times, meanwhile opting for more efficient smaller transport? Groceries are usually no trouble to carry in any size automobile.

Sit down and think of where you use the car. Mostly in short trips, with an occasional trip of more than 150 miles, and maybe once a year a long one of 500 to 2,000 miles? That's an average use profile. Your choice also depends upon where this is being done—in the mountains, on flat sweeping superhighways, or in the city. If you go on dirt or gravel with plenty of inclines and tight curves, you should opt for a larger engine, extra-duty suspension, and the best tires you can afford, but still buying the smallest vehicle that fits your needs.

If you plan to maintain the vehicle yourself, you should be able to figure out that any vehicle with a very crowded engine compartment is going to be a terror to work on. We have rejected cars that seemed too difficult to maintain, but those who will be letting George the mechanic do it need not worry.

19

Buying for Durability | Before making the choice final, you have an additional factor to consider. That is durability. There is likely to be more than one make that can fill the bill, and perhaps as many as five or six. Don't foreclose on any of them until you have investigated all of them. To make this a bit easier, you can first make a preliminary elimination. If your choice includes a Ford and a Mercury, pick one. If your choice includes a Chevy, Buick, Olds, and Pontiac model, pick one. If your choice includes Chrysler-Dodge or Plymouth-Dodge, pick one. Why? All similar cars made by a single manufacturer are the same basic units with changes in sheet metal, in interior trim, and sometimes (rarely) in a significant interior dimension.

How should you choose? You should pick on the basis of the styling you prefer, the dealer you prefer (both in terms of proximity and service reputation), the flexibility of use, and the comparative price and value. By all means get the best financing deal and insurance deal, but when you are going to keep a car seven to ten years or longer, superior seating, a larger fuel tank, a slightly better bumper and protection system, or more comfortable seat belts should be worth more to you than a slight advantage in financing.

Durability involves the shaping of the vehicle. Are there poorly protected impact-prone areas—sides, fender caps, wheel openings, grilles, tail plates? If you live in a city, are there sturdy rub strips and bumper guards? If the lips of some wheel openings protrude, are they protected?

Durability also involves how the car is made. If, for instance, moldings and seams are crooked when the car is in showroom condition, what can you expect later? If you think that the seats look shoddy, that makes them shoddy. Look at the door hinges. Test the door by swinging it gently back and forth with a finger, before gently pushing it closed. If it doesn't swing and close easily in the showroom model, what's it going to do six years hence? Also, remember that the wider the door, the bigger the hinges, and the harder to keep it perfectly aligned.

There are two basic kinds of car construction—a *frame*

with a *body* attached, and a *unit body*. The latter is built so that the body itself is the structure (also called *unitized* or *monococque* construction). Either can be durable, but if you have a history of minor fender-benders, you are better off with frame-and-body. Unit construction costs more to repair, and needs to be rustproofed and soundproofed more thoroughly. But it is likely to be squeakfree and stronger in a major accident.

Durability involves the controls—both their positioning and their quality. Door-opening mechanisms, seat-adjustment levers, light switches, wiper controls, and all pedals need to be examined. How many turns does it take to open a side window? (Electric windows fall into the area of extra complexity.) And what about door and trunk locks? Some trunk lids have shoddy locks.

Durability also involves simplicity. Any extra convenience that you add makes the car more complex. That doesn't mean you shouldn't get power steering; it means you should get power steering on cars that require it, but not on subcompacts or on well-balanced compacts. That doesn't mean that you don't buy automatic transmission where you have a choice; it means that you may buy it if you need it because you do a great deal of stop-and-go driving, but you realize that you will be paying the penalty in fuel. Durability doesn't mean you forget about air conditioning; it means that you buy it only if you live where only air conditioning will make driving bearable for significant parts of the year.

And durability involves use. You don't buy white velour interiors if you are commuting to construction sites or if you have small, chocolate-loving offspring.

Durability involves making the decision to protect whatever new car you buy from the beginning. We feel that the rust-perforation warranties of the companies are not sufficient and that you will need to get additional rust-proofing, either as a dealer option (which has the advantage of being included in your new-car financing if you don't have extra cash) or in the aftermarket. We also would opt for paint protection, both because the dealer will then do a better car-prep job and because you will have him two ways on paint defects.

You should buy mats for the carpeting, and you should also make sure that the spark plugs have protective rubber covers and that there are mud and stone guards on the trailing edges of the wheel openings.

Finally, durability involves getting information, either from reading material or from an expert, and weighing its value intelligently when you make your choices.

The other key thing to do—with either a new or a used car—is to call the National Highway Traffic Safety Administration Recall Hotline (800–424–9393) to find out if recent models of the car you are considering have been recalled. If so, for what? Check that particular item.

Once you have purchased the vehicle of your choice, if not of your fantasies, the struggle for preservation begins. Upon signing the order, let the salesman and the dealer know that you will examine the vehicle minutely when you take delivery and that you will not accept the vehicle if it needs repairs or adjustments. Suggest that when the dealer thinks it is prepped, he should call you so you can make a predelivery inspection. *Never inspect a car at night unless you are under lights so bright the local surgeon could perform an operation on the spot.* Never take delivery of a car at night. Do everything in broad daylight, and do it methodically. Bring friends or relatives to look over the paint job and to do other inspections that take nothing but common sense and good eyesight.

What else do you inspect?

Why don't you start at the rear bumper and move forward, inspecting methodically? It may have an effect on your vehicle's life span. If the bumper has a rub strip, make sure it has no bubbles. Make sure there are no scratches on the bumper itself. Finally before moving on, inspect the area under the rear bumper for serious defects in the paint.

Go over the paint carefully on the entire car. Four double-checking eyes are better than two. Runs, drip residue, large nicks, and scratches should all be remedied by the dealer.

Check the window glass. It should be free of the tiny scratches that produce a hazy glare in twilight or in the bright sun. There also should be no imperfections inside the glass, such as tiny bubbles.

Check underneath the car. This area should look clean and new. If it doesn't, get an explanation. Common ones are: "We road-tested it," "That happened in shipping," and "It was parked in an auxiliary lot." Depending upon how dirty it is, accept or refuse the car. If it's very dirty, it may mean that it was a demo or rental model and the odometer was altered. This is rare, because it's illegal in all states and not worth the scandal.

Check the tires for inflation and the wheels for the patina of newness. Tire treads should still have the tiny knobs of rubber that signify that they're new. It's rare, but sometimes the dealer has the occasion to switch on a set of slightly used tires and use the new ones elsewhere.

Check the doors. See if they swing easily on the hinges. You should be able to close them with a slight push of your finger. See if the hinges were lubricated. You are now working on the inside, so go back to the trunk and see if the lid opens and closes easily. Make sure that if there is a trunk lining, it is installed properly. Make sure that all wires you can see are out of the way. Make sure that the tool kit and the proper spare are present and in place.

In the passenger compartment, inspect the seats, the carpeting, and the side panels for either bad fit or defects. Inspect especially how decorative moldings are installed; do not accept a vehicle where the moldings are too short, crooked, or misaligned. Look at the door sill to see how it has been installed: no missing screws. Look at the fit of the doors from the inside: no ugly gaps. Look especially at the rubber or cloth-covered stripping around either the door or the door opening. It should fit tightly. If any paint shows, make sure that there are no drips or other irregularities.

Try everything you can from the ashtray and glove-box

door to the seat adjustments, windshield washer and wiper, and signals. Take your time: this is the most important inspection that you will ever make of this car. It will go reasonably fast if, as we suggested, you have others helping you. If the salesman or service adviser displays impatience, ignore it. After all, he's getting your money.

Looking under the hood will tell you only if it is a new car or if it is a masked version of one of many forms of used unit, like an "executive car" or "press car" or even "demo." The vast majority of dealers will be honest about giving you this information, but misinformation needs to happen only once to give you a bad buy, financially if not mechanically.

In a good new-car delivery service, the salesperson will offer or insist upon a familiarization ride, during which he or she checks to make sure you know how to operate the various features of the vehicle. If he or she doesn't offer, ask for this service, because you want to have him present if you find any defects in the vehicle while it's moving. (Having two or three others with you will approximate a full load and more clearly indicate real performance.) The ride should include a few blocks of bumpy road or cross railroad tracks, and it should include a hill, if possible. If you think any detail of performance is poor, tell him then. Don't be put off by assurances that "We'll repair anything later; the car is under warranty." Don't take delivery until the car works and *is as perfect* as you want it to be! You have warned the dealer that this would happen and he or she should believe you.

Unless the car-buying public—that's you—holds dealers and car companies to strict quality standards, it will continue to receive less-than-perfect new vehicles that passed some goof-off inspector at the factory and then the "get ready" of a dealer who does little more than wash the car and take the crayon marks off the window. Dealers are paid preparation money by the car maker or distributor, to make a series of checks of the new car; some try to skimp on this and "steal" the prep money. Certainly the personnel in "make ready" or "get ready"—the name of the department that preps new cars—tends to be from the lower echelon of help at many dealerships. So the final responsibility for inspection is yours.

The second phase of making your new car into a vehicle that should last is the warranty period. During this time you should correct shortcomings that you perceive, or get explanations that satisfy you.

Of course, you must be fair about it. If you bought a heavy car with a four-cylinder engine, you can't expect sparkling performance. If you specified one of the few remaining V-8s, you should not expect 30-mpg fuel economy. The EPA gas mileage numbers do not obtain for every driving style and environment. They are now slightly more realistic than they were before the 1981 model year. Complain only if you are missing the number for your vehicle by a wide margin—more than 4 mpg. Then it may be a symptom of either poor adjustment or malfunction of components in the powertrain.

And you certainly can't expect a full repaint job because you discover a single nick.

We believe that most surviving dealers want to do right by you; sometimes the dealership owner is not aware of customer dissatisfaction. Some dealers own two, three, or even seven dealerships and don't sell anymore. You need to voice your problems to them, and the only way is to write to them. But complain only after giving lower-echelon personnel a chance. You wouldn't want people going over your head until you had tried to satisfy them, would you?

We also believe that you should try to have a pleasant relationship with the dealer. You need not be belligerent about telling what you believe is wrong with the car; just be businesslike. We believe many people are dissatisfied unnecessarily, because they don't bother to communicate with the dealer. They think it's hopeless to do so, but it is not. The squeaky wheel gets the grease: that is all too true in our society, the first economic system to run by complaint.

4
Driving to Save Your Car

It's amazing how few people realize that their driving style affects how long their automobile will last and the cost of operating it. You take two people, each driving about 14,000 miles of mostly city and suburban roads a year. Let's call one Fast Harry and the other Economy Smith. Old Fast Harry is hitting the brakes about four times the rate of Economy Smith and is straining every moving part in the power-train each time he accelerates from a stop-light or any standing start. He's making the suspension work like a demon each time he whips around a corner like a runaway Jake Kochman Hell Driver doing a rim ride with two wheels in the air. Not only that, Fast Harry is using 40 percent more of that liquid money called gasoline with his driving habits, and he is much more likely to contribute to the $3.5 billion auto-accident industry.

But what about old Economy Smith? Is he necessarily a good driver? Well, it depends. Our ideal in this case is not to know how to slide a vehicle through curves in the quickest possible manner. There is a national 55-mph speed limit, which might make that a bit chancy on any given day in any given locale. Our ideal is to use the vehicle as efficiently as possible so that

> We get where we're going in good time.
>
> We don't "Fast Harry" the vehicle's running and stopping systems into an early demise.
>
> We avoid accidents, which after all are the number-one reason for junking a car.

There are perhaps a hundred books telling about proper driving technique, and we still think the British police drivers' manual, *Roadcraft,* is as good as they come. If you really want to elevate common ordinary commuter-type driving to an art, you should get a British friend to buy this thin 77-page book for you. But laying out the finer points of driving technique is not our purpose. Instead, you must look at yourself as the ultimate control mechanism in the machinery that transports you. In other words, if you are driving properly, you are concentrating and making judgments that further your purpose—to pass smoothly, with minimum effect, and at the least cost to you and the environment to your destination.

There's another angle to driving that dovetails with this: drive as if you were an economy-run contestant, because gasoline is becoming as precious as twenty-year-old Scotch.

Once upon a time there was a sales promotion called the Mobil Economy Run. It was so magnificent it transcended its original purpose and became a classic American competition. It was finally laid to rest in 1968, when economy was a dirty word in Detroit and the average speed of the run from California to New York was more than 50 mph.

But the drivers, experts all, still used economy techniques to wring every possible bit of mileage out of vehicles whose construction had as much relation to economy as lard to unleavened Passover bread. The techniques are simple, but they are boring and can be tiring to people learning them. They include the following:

- Avoid fast acceleration, not only in jackrabbit starts but in all normal driving. Emergencies are exceptions, but you can minimize the likelihood of their occurrence if you leave yourself thinking time by concentrating on your driving environment.

- Stay off the brakes. Use them as seldom and as lightly as possible. This is the single most important technique you can learn. Brakes waste the momentum your car has built up. In all driving, try hard to match your speed to traffic speed. Many times this is impossible, but at least try. By avoiding sudden stops, you save more than through most of the expensive mechanical modifications to save fuel.

- Try to keep a steady foot on the accelerator. According to Mobil, tests show that a constant speed can save 7 to 9 percent of the petrol used by old Fast Harry, whose speed varies over a range of 5 mph.

- Drive as smoothly as possible by anticipating traffic as much as a quarter of a mile away in the city and as far as you can see on highways.

- Avoid unnecessary engine idling. In cold weather a car is "warmed up" enough to drive in about a minute. When you are stalled in a traffic jam more than three minutes, turn off the engine.

Mobil ran an experiment to test whether ordinary drivers could improve their gas mileage if taught economy-run techniques. The answer in a nutshell was yes, sometimes by 3 or 4 mpg. They utilized an accessory, a vacuum gauge attached to the intake manifold, to help the participants realize they wasted gas by their driving style. A vacuum monitored the volume of air-fuel mixture going through the carburetor into the intake manifold and thence into the combustion chamber.

You, too, can easily buy and install this device. If you pay attention to it, you'll notice when you are driving economically and when you are wasting gasoline. Mount it as near your normal line of vision as possible without obstructing anything else, so that your eye can detect needle variations without neglecting the view up ahead. The gauge will be very responsive to accelerator-pedal tap dancers —people who don't exert a smooth, even pressure. If you take it seriously, you will find yourself driving more evenly and receiving more miles for each gallon of gas.

Mobil Economy Run veterans claim you learn to "feel" manifold pressure after a while, suggesting that the gauge is a sort of training instrument. It's also a nuisance if it's always running with the needle in the red and you know that means you're blowing your money out the rear end. Eventually you adapt and become hooked on good driving techniques. That includes keeping speeds down. We won't mention the average 27 percent fuel saving in U.S. cars by dropping from 70 to 50 mph. How much saving that really is in dollars depends on your car, but look at Appendix Two to get an idea.

There are special driving situations—driving in the wintry North, driving in the mountains, and gamesmanship in the city. None of them negates anything we've said so far except that some people may consider what goes on in big cities to be an exercise more in parking than in driving.

The gist of the whole matter is whether you're going to think that you are a good driver because you have nothing closer than near misses and know how to get that car moving at top speed, or whether you're willing to try to assess yourself critically. We have a test (see page 30). If you lie about it, you hurt only yourself.

	Often	Some-times	Hardly Ever	Never
	(5 points)	(3 points)	(1 point)	(0 points)
Jackrabbit starts				
Don't signal before changing lane				
Don't signal before turning (every time)				
Park by bump and feel				
One-hand driving (tell the truth)				
Ride the brake pedal (rest foot lightly)				
Ride the clutch				
Smoke while driving				
Argue while driving				
Don't check side and rear mirrors before changing lane				
Speed regularly fluctuates 5 mph, even in light traffic				
Don't check to keep under posted speed				
Tailgate to move a slower car over				
Ride shoulder to pass on inside				
Let driving become competition				
Lose temper at another car (no matter what)				
Become engrossed in radio				
Become engrossed in conversation				
Drive with obscured windshield or obscured side windows				
Drive after more than one drink				

If you score 100, please turn in your driver's license voluntarily. You are temperamentally unsuited to the operation of an automobile anywhere except in a Dodg'em game or a demolition derby. If you score 60 or more, please examine your driving style at once; it's shortening the life of the vehicle and it may shorten yours. Excellent drivers score under 45—unless they score under 20, in which case we are reasonably sure they are lying.

Jackrabbit starts, bump-and-feel parking, riding the brake or clutch, competition, and angered driving all directly affect the wear and tear on the vehicle. The others all contribute to accidents.

There is just one other large area that directly affects the life of the car and the well-being of you and yours. That is road strategy. You know pretty well all the shortcuts and problems in getting from where you live to where you work, for instance. You probably found out by trial and error. That's the hard way, and it's not practical to drive to new places either on business or vacation that way. Get into the habit of planning all trips to unfamiliar places, no matter how near. Take into account that the type of road can cost you gas. With an asphalt highway as the base, a potholed or much-patched road may cost up to 15 percent fuel penalty and stretches of loose gravel up to 35 percent.

1) Use the telephone. Call the people you are visiting to find what they think is the best way to get there. Get exact street names for the route. Get the exact street address of where you're supposed to end up if it's a home or commercial building. Get landmarks close by.

2) If you belong to AAA (American Automobile Association), check for estimated travel time and learn whether there is any obstruction on your route.

3) Getting lost wastes gas and can put unnecessary wear on the car. Don't be afraid to call the town police for directions if you think you're lost. You don't know what town? Dial the operator after you get a street, highway name, or even a business name, and ask for the police, then explain.

4) Plan longer trips (like vacations) in great detail —where you're going to make your gas stops, your refreshment stops, your overnight stops. Book motels in advance or as early as possible in the day. If there are small children involved, figure on extra stops.

5) The higher your traveling speed, the more rest stops you as driver will need, even if you have an automatic speed control. Add rest stops also if you're driving at night, in inclement weather, or with hazardous road conditions. Try to combine stops— getting fuel, visiting rest rooms, picking up food or eating, making phone calls, switching drivers. There's no way a family with small children can do all these things only once in a trip of over 150 miles, but healthy adults can.

6) If you're solo driving a long distance in a hurry, don't overdrive. We pounded from New York to Denver once in 49 hours before the 55-mph speed limit, and Providence must have been with us. But we did pull far off the road for two catnaps, and each time we stopped for gas we did stretching exercises and washed our face and arms. If you're from the crowded East or near Midwest and never tried driving across the Great Plains, you have no concept of what you're attempting. Take a plane. If you're from the Plains and have never driven in the Boston-to-Washington corridor, you had better be prepared for claustrophobia, especially in the center of cities anywhere along the route.

7) One of the keys to longer life for your automobile is that it, too, must be prepared for longer trips. Check tires for proper pressure and make a complete check under the hood before starting.

8) For long trips we always pack eyewash solution and window cleaner. Eyestrain is a major ingredient in road fatigue; keep the windshield and rear windows spotless. We also carry four Wash'n Dries per person per 150 miles. Sometimes they're better than air conditioning, which incidentally we use as sparingly as possible. They could make air conditioners that don't cut 10 percent off your gas mileage, but they haven't yet.

9) If at all possible, we fill up the tank and *personally* check under the hood each time the fuel needle goes between the half or, at most, the quarter-full mark. But if you know the route, the location of the filling stations and approximately how fast your vehicle guzzles gas, you can plan your road strategy for fewer stops.

10) If you miscalculate on gas and realize it in time, slow to about 35 mph and drive at a steady pace (in the right lane, please). This is about as efficient a speed as there is for your engine. If you don't make it, pull well over to the side of the road and put out your distress signals. But no one who plans ahead should ever run out of gas!

One last driving note: if you find that on even stretches of road with little traffic you can't hold the vehicle at a steady speed with fluctuations of less than 3 mph, most likely you are tiring and should rest. Some drivers have never learned to drive at a steady speed; they are hazards to everyone else, whether they are fluctuating between 35 and 40 mph or 65 and 70.

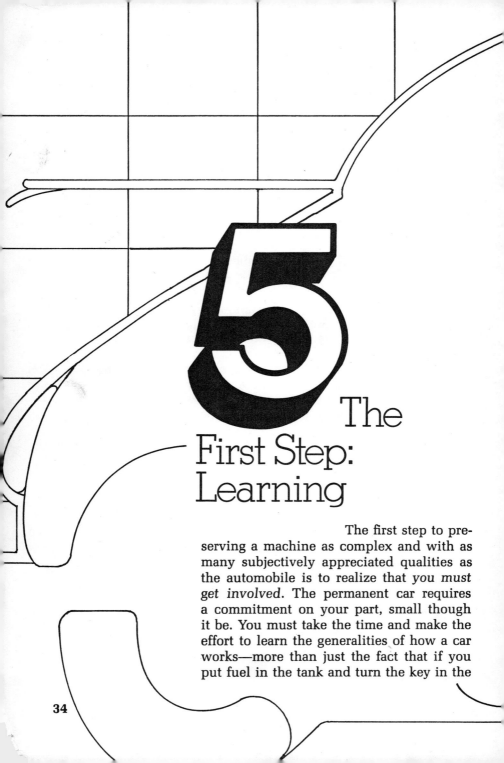

5

The First Step: Learning

The first step to preserving a machine as complex and with as many subjectively appreciated qualities as the automobile is to realize that *you must get involved*. The permanent car requires a commitment on your part, small though it be. You must take the time and make the effort to learn the generalities of how a car works—more than just the fact that if you put fuel in the tank and turn the key in the starter, the engine starts and that somehow makes the car go.

Appendix One at the back of this book gives you the basics. Read it. Try checking it out against your car. Ask people questions.

Even if you never turn a screw, you must make decisions about repairing and refurbishing the car. You used to be able to avoid these decisions when you traded the car in, because many of the choices hadn't arisen yet. But with a permanent car, you need to be at least a little familiar with its workings now or you leave yourself open to ripoffs later.

The commitment usually extends to periodic expenditure of elbow grease, although you can minimize that by several methods, not the least of which is having others do the work. There is something to be said for large, well-run families, especially if there are kids in the car-nut phase who will do the work. But you cannot escape the periodic need to inspect the car and maintain it as necessary. This is the very least you can do.

With that said, we now can begin to see what can be done to keep the vehicle well and running. Let's get things organized, so that as we intensify our efforts to make the car closer to being permanent we have a basic procedure. This is a priority plan, but you must modify any or all parts of it according to your driving style and according to where and what you drive.

PRIORITY ONE: ENGINE FLUIDS

Keeping a machine cooled, greased, and oiled according to its needs is far and away the most important single action you can take to preserve it and protect it from costly major repairs.

Here are the usual places you must service and the *maximum* intervals for most cars 1977 and younger (see table on following page).

Remember we said these were maximum intervals. If you check your owner's manual, you'll see it refers to cars "in normal service." It is likely that your driving falls at least

Kind	Action	Maximum Interval
Engine oil	Change	7,500 miles
Antifreeze-coolant	Change	One year
Brake fluid	Inspect	One month
Transmission fluid	Inspect	Four months
Windshield-washer fluid	Add antifreeze type before winter	

in some seasons into what the car makers themselves call "severe conditions." What are "severe conditions"? Many trips of 6 miles or less qualify as severe driving conditions. Driving in dusty areas regularly is a severe condition. Towing a trailer is a severe condition. Extended operation at high speed and any operation with a maximum load are severe conditions. So are extended idling and stop-and-go driving.

The AAA claims that more than 60 percent of all automobile trips are 6 miles long or less. Check your own driving pattern, because engine oil needs 10 to 15 miles to reach proper operating temperature in most cars. If you are a commuter, most likely you do plenty of stop-and-go driving and your vehicle sits and idles almost daily. Dust is a constant problem in some places, and we might add that industrial pollution poses a problem, too.

The recommendations change radically for severe conditions (see table on next page).

Engine Oil | It would seem obvious that you are recommended to change the engine oil sooner either because the oil loses its qualities or because it becomes dirty. Both are partially true. The whole subject of oil can get very technical, more so than may interest you. But since it is the single most important act of preventive maintenance, you need to know why it is so important.

Kind	Action	Maximum Interval
Engine oil	Change	3,000 miles
Antifreeze-coolant	Change	Six months (spring and fall)
Brake fluid	Inspect	One month
Transmission fluid	Inspect	One month

The engine is composed of many moving parts machined to fit very closely together. If these parts are dry, the surfaces will bind and stop the engine from running. This is called *seizing*. The first function of the oil is to provide an interface, sometimes only a few molecules thick, between the metal parts so that the parts can mesh without seizing. This is *lubrication*.

But that is only one function. Car engines by nature create great internal heat. The antifreeze-coolant carries much of this heat away and gets rid of it via the radiator. The oil also removes heat as it circulates and thus it must be able to withstand the heat it is transporting.

And, finally, in most modern engines the oil acts as a cleaner and an antisludge agent. Detergent oils remove carbon, pollutants, and anything else from inner engine surfaces and transport them out.

Faced with all these requirements, oil manufacturers produce a wide variety of motor oils graded as to service and weight. We will not attempt to describe all the various gradations. You need to know only a few things about this part of the subject: what service ratings mean and what the difference is between single- and multi-weight oils. (The manufacturers usually tell you about the additives they put in, too. The additives are there for good reasons—some make the oil tougher, others make it more slippery. It is the additives that eventually break down and actually change the rating of your oil from adequate to inadequate protection.)

The American Petroleum Institute has a series of *service classifications* for various uses. For instance, farm-vehicle usage is different from car use. All you need to remember is to buy only SE or SF classified oil (the classification is embossed into the oil can and/or printed on the label). Oil *weight* or *lubricity* ratings are a little trickier, because they depend on the outside temperature. The weight or lubricity rating gives an indication as to how easily the oil will flow: the higher the number, the slower the flow. For instance, a 40W or 50W oil has more body (is heavier and thicker) than a 5W oil. It will flow more slowly but it will be able to lubricate at a higher temperature. Thus, if you were using a single-weight oil in a climate where the temperatures were consistently below freezing, you might use 10W oil, but in the spring when things warmed up, you would move to 30W or 40W.

Multi-grade or multi-lubricity oils are formulated to operate over a wider temperature range, permitting you to leave them in longer. In very cold regions you can buy 5W–30 so the oil can flow into the cold engine quickly, offering little resistance to the starting mode. In more temperate climes, 10W–30 or even 10W–40 permits operation from 0° to 85° or 100°F. respectively. In Southern areas 20W–40 or 20W–50 protects from 15° to 100°F.

If you are using the correct weight oil, the next question is, How long can you expect this oil to do its job? Does it really break down? As we noted, the answer is that oil itself never breaks down, which is why commercial companies can take what is drained out of the crankcases of America and re-refine it. (Re-refined oil is used in nonconsumer vehicles.) The oil in your crankcase, however, becomes polluted and diluted and its additives lose their effectiveness. Airborne contaminants can enter the engine through the oil-fill pipe, even through the dipstick hole or an ineffective oil filter. Blowby gases sneak past inside the engine. Water or condensation sneaks in, and suddenly the oil is less effective despite your oil filter. Severe driving conditions, especially, shorten oil life. What has happened to the oil is that it is dirty and the additives have deteriorated so that what was 10W–40 when new may be 10W–20 after 3,000 miles. There is degradation of both detergent action and resistance to heat and pollution.

As a practitioner of preventive maintenance, what you should do is to err on the side of caution if you err at all. For instance, if you change oil every 3,000 miles and drive 12,000 miles in a year, you can change for every season. That would permit switching oil weights by season and using single-grade oil. But living in New Jersey, we prefer multi-grade oils for the added protection against sudden temperature change.

Well, what about those 25,000-mile synthetic oils, and other oils supposed to last for 15,000 miles? Read the cans or containers. None recommend use beyond one year, so suddenly we are cut down to whatever distance you cover in a year. And you will also note that such oils are always more expensive than excellent-grade brand-name oils of the same lubricity ratings—even, often, the same brand name. These oils are formulated to stand up to 15,000 or 25,000 miles of use, but if you drive less than the rated distance, you aren't getting the full benefit for the added cost, and the ad claims don't apply to you.

If you decide that you'll try an oil-change interval of 5,000 miles or less, we fail to see how these superpremium oils can be justified. But most claim increased mpg. If you drive 12,000 miles a year and you believe their claims of extra mpg, we feel you would need to get at least two extra miles per gallon to justify the cost differential alone. Another consideration is whether the oil filter you choose can keep these oils clean over that period.

There are other exclusions. You are wasting your money if you buy synthetic or even superpremium oil for a rotary-engined Mazda, the only rotary in mass production. The rotary engine is designed to burn oil to cool itself. Thus, a reasonably good conventional oil—single weight—should do just as well. For conventional engines in extreme temperature conditions, however, synthetics may well be justified.

They let the engine start easier when it's below 0°F., and they resist extreme heat like constant readings above 99°F.

As to separate oil additives, that's a subject we'll take up later.

Antifreeze-Coolant | Antifreeze-coolant—meaning a product based on ethylene glycol—makes your life easier, assuming you read the directions for protection at various temperatures that are on most containers. If you are having someone do the installation and removal, make very clear the temperature range for which you wish to have protection. He will use more or less according to what you say.

Some people, however, still use straight water, or water and alcohol, as their coolant. They face a problem that even those using ethylene-glycol solutions face, but it is much magnified. Depending on where they live, the water contains more or fewer minerals. Mineral water is great for people but not so good for radiators, where the minerals can build into a residue and also can react chemically with the copper in the radiators. So users of straight water should clean and flush the radiator at least winter and summer and should use an anticorrosion solution. The alcohol is usually added in cold weather to inhibit freezing.

The ethylene-glycol solutions are generally superior for three reasons:

- They boil at a higher temperature.

- They lower the freezing point if used in proper solution (never use 100 percent glycol; its freezing point is 12°F., yet with 50 percent water the freezing point is 0°F.).

- They contain rust inhibitors and conditioners, which act to neutralize contaminants, including the mineral content of the water in the solution.

The severe-service recommendation for flushes and refills before winter and summer relates to the fact that the conditioners (not the ethylene glycol itself) tend to become less effective under heat and use. Incidentally, it is the water pump rather than the radiator or hoses that is usually the link in the cooling system most likely to malfunction and that necessitates some of these conditioners.

Unless you live in a hard-water area and use the hard water, we tend to believe that antifreeze-coolants have been improved enough to make it through the year. A very few cars have been produced in the past with sealed cooling systems; these employ distilled water with glycol, as far as we can ascertain.

Sure, you probably know of people who never change the coolant. These people will pass their troubles to the next owner—but remember, you are trying to make your car as close to permanent as possible with minimum cost. Antifreeze-coolant is less expensive than a new or rebuilt radiator, a water pump or, in an extreme case, work in the engine on the water jackets. If you have experienced the inconvenience of boilover, at that time you would have given much more than the cost of a radiator flush and refill just to rejoin the stop-and-go traffic in which it probably happened.

Brake Fluid | Brake fluid is trickier than either engine oil or antifreeze-coolant. On many U.S. cars, particularly older ones, it is difficult to check brake fluid, but most imports and some late-model U.S. cars provide a visible reservoir in the engine compartment.

The most important point about brake fluid is that it must be uncontaminated by either dirt or air. If the fluid is dirty, the entire hydraulic brake system must be flushed. If you see many air bubbles, see a brake service and find out why.

You also need to keep brake fluid topped off with the exact liquid specified in your owner's manual. Brake fluid, especially with disk brakes, must face temperatures of 500°F. and more, as it absorbs heat from friction. If you have a bad habit of resting your left foot on the brake pedal while driving, you are courting disaster, especially if your car has disk brakes. Stop the habit at once. With disk brakes, this slight pedal pressure keeps the disk in contact with the caliper, thus wearing the pad unnecessarily, creating heat and wasting gas.

Transmission Fluid | Transmission fluid is something hardly anyone checks, even in the garage business. Check it at least every 9,000 miles—read the owner's manual to find out how. Usually there is a separate dipstick.

Differential Oil | And, finally, did you ever see the garage man unscrew a bolt in the differential in the rear of your car when it was on a lift and then stick in his pinky? He's checking oil level. Top this up if needed with the oil recommended in the owner's manual. Or have it done.

Windshield Washer Fluid | Windshield washer fluid can be bought so inexpensively that it pays to use it instead of water. It often contains a mild detergent to clean the window better and an antifreeze for winter use.

Employ the windshield washer any time you see the window is dirty or dusty—few people utilize it enough. When the "squirt" starts to become anemic, it's time to refill.

Also make sure the squirt pattern is hitting the window properly. Your dealer will tell you how to adjust it if the information is not in the owner's manual.

Use Owner's Manual | By now you may have gotten the idea that the owner's manual is vital. It is, because it contains information specific to your automobile. You wouldn't try to put up a children's swing without directions, so how can you expect to maintain your car without the manufacturer's specifications and recommendations?

Even if you think you know a great deal about cars in general, it is a good idea to walk yourself through the car with the owner's manual as your guide. Then walk anyone else involved with the car through. Some owner's manuals will test even the most knowledgeable when you get to the troubleshooting part. You should identify for yourself or your confreres the location of each possible cause of a given malady. All this need not be done at one time; spread the joy of new knowledge.

PRIORITY TWO: FILTERS

Smokey Yunick, one of the most famous of the builders of racing stock cars, says that changing the various oils and filters at least as often as manufacturers specify and more likely much more often is the number-one activity he recommends to people who want to keep their cars a long time. He is inherently suspicious of 7,500-mile-oil intervals with petroleum-based oil and wonders if you can really justify the cost of synthetic oil unless you have especially severe or erratic weather conditions. Which is just what we said previously.

Yunick feels that filters are as important—almost—as the fluids you put in and advises that you do what is necessary to monitor them. There are a variety of filters on the car, which require different actions. They include the filters listed in the table on the following page.

Oil Filter

This filter is positioned so that all oil flows through it before reaching close-tolerance parts like the piston rings, engine bearings, cylinder walls, and ultimately the crankshaft. That system is called a full-flow system, since the oil must be cleansed of contaminants continuously; trucks use a bypass system, where only some of the oil is filtered first. There are two general types of oil filters and many that combine attributes of the types. Relying on the fact that modern engine oils contain additives that prevent the buildup of sludge, many manufacturers use a surface-type

Kind	Action	Maximum Interval
Oil filter	Replace	9,000 miles
Fuel filter (gas line)	Replace	12,000 miles
Air filter element	Inspect, clean Replace	3,000 miles One year
Transmission filter	Inspect, clean	9,000 miles
Emissions filters	Inspect, clean Replace	6,000 miles 15,000 miles

filter medium, usually pleated paper. This type of filter catches dirt and abrasive particles down to a certain size in the same way a sieve catches any ingredient larger than the size of its mesh. Finer particles, presumably too fine to do damage, will fall through.

But Ford, in particular, uses a depth-type filter, which works on an entirely different principle. This is a canister of packed cotton batting with synthetic-fiber mesh below. The idea here is that the cotton will catch particles five to ten times finer than the pleated paper-type elements as they work through the cotton batting and the different fibers of the nylon mesh. Depth-type filters, however, offer more resistance to oil flow, and since they catch more they tend to get dirty and clog quicker.

When a filter clogs, there is a pressure-relief valve, usually in the filter itself, which opens and lets unfiltered oil flow through. That is why you need to change oil filters at least according to manufacturers' recommendations, and sooner for severe service. It will clog quicker these days than in the old days, which were before people worried about emissions and before tolerances became closer to control those emissions or to get more efficient burning of the fuel.

We mentioned the oil could be contaminated, diluted, and polluted by air contaminants, blowby gases, and water

44

from condensation or leakage. The oil filter also must deal with the metal particles from the wear of bearings, pistons, even cylinder walls, as well as foundry core sand still hiding from the engine casting. Either type of filter can usually handle these if it is relatively fresh.

What you need to remember is that the filter must be changed according to your driving conditions. Switching away from the type of filter used by your manufacturer to what you may consider an improved type made by someone else is perfectly permissible. But regard with a beady eye any filter that says "Never Change Your Oil Again" or some such trash. It's probably even less effective than the rig one company once sold—a canister into which you inserted a roll of toilet paper as the filter element. The toilet paper filtered until it clogged up, which was relatively quickly. Then you were supposed to toss out the oil-clogged toilet paper and insert a fresh roll, blithely tossing out all the oil in the toilet paper. That idea didn't make it; neither did the filter using a permanent medium of tiny metal pellets.

There is a device on the market at this writing that we frankly haven't tested. It contains an ultra-fine (3-micron) disposable filter, a heating element to keep oil within the filter unit at 200°F., and a vent hole. The contaminants in the oil are supposed to vaporize and go up the vent, leaving the oil pure so you need never change it. It's patented. We mention it in case you wish to investigate.

For now we shall continue to change the oil and, given a conventional filter, we think the interval of change is more important. We consider owner's-manual recommendations as maximum.

Oils on the market containing graphite or Teflon or molybdenum disulfide may require a specific oil filter. If you use such oils, follow the recommendation of whoever markets the oil as to filter. It's likely that a surface type might work but you would need to check out depth types and combinations. There are also many oil additives ranging from STP to PTFE (fluorocarbons). Most claim greatly increased lubricating properties. If you use these products check *their* recommendations as to filter and follow *their* directions as to use. If you alter oil-change intervals because of them, at least change the *filter* regularly. We suppose you could drain the oil containing your elixir into a container, change the filter, and reinstall the oil, topping it off if necessary with new oil. (We believe that a product containing fluorocarbons can help save fuel in older cars. But you must follow their directions exactly. If you do not, you may use *more* gas, because the idle speed must be readjusted downward after the product conquers some of the friction.)

Air Filter **|** Your car runs mainly on air. For every gallon of gasoline or gasohol about 1,000 gallons of air will be gulped by the carburetor. That is a great deal of air and tells quickly why the air filter is so important. The air filter element is housed in that circular thing atop the motor that has a cover held on by a wing nut. (Don't lose that wing nut when you unscrew it to inspect the filter element!)

The air filter does what it says. It removes dust, dirt, salt, industrial pollution, and pollen from the air before the carburetor swallows it. In a very dusty area, for instance, you may need to inspect and clean the air filter daily. Why? Because if the air filter clogs you can lose 2 to 3 mpg or find that your vehicle's engine is missing on one or more cylinders, losing power, backfiring, or starting hard.

It is amazing how many people get sucked into possibly expensive repairs to cure missing or hard starting or low gas mileage, when all they need to do is keep that air filter element clean and, if it is the most common type—pleated paper between two pieces of screening—replace it when cleaning still leaves it dirty-looking. We're not saying that there aren't other causes for hard starting and the other problems mentioned—obviously there are—but a clogged air filter should *never* be one of them.

There are a number of variations on the dry type of air-filter element claiming various degrees of durability. We have described the standard one. Another kind utilizes both pleated paper and a batting; it claims that smaller particles are caught and the element will last longer. Still another type utilizes oil-wetted pleated paper for claimed greater efficiency, and another combines wrapping with oil-wetted paper.

For some years General Motors has claimed it has been using a permanent air-filter element. That doesn't mean GM owners can forget about it; it means they need to inspect it and vacuum it off at least every 2,500 miles. The dry-type filters all can be vacuumed; those with oil-wetted paper cannot.

Some race cars use a foamed plastic (like polyurethane) called Filtron to catch even the tiniest impurities. We are told it is impractical for passenger-car use over a long period. You must judge how clean or dirty or salty or whatever the environment is where you are driving the car. Then inspect, clean, or change the air filter accordingly. If you drive through an exceptionally dusty area, it's so easy to check the filter that you ought to do it that very day.

Gasoline Filter | The fuel filters on some General Motors models are permanent, located inside the gas tank. We are interested in the kind that is replaceable. Usually, these are inserted somewhere along the fuel line. There likely is one in your car, whatever the manufacturer, for safety reasons. A federal safety standard limits the amount of fuel that may leak out after a car has rolled over, so many fuel filters have a check valve that shuts tight when the car is upside down.

But the fuel filter has equally important—and more constant—duties in ensuring the purity of the gas that gets to the carburetor. The rust and water from condensation in the vehicle's fuel tank are two possible sources of fuel contamination, but the fuel may also have picked up contaminants on its long journey from the refinery to the gas station.

There are too many types of fuel filter to describe. We prefer the clear plastic type, because you can just look in and see if it's doing anything, but others certainly can do the job. When they clog, the gasoline finally can't make it through;

then perhaps the car won't start, or the engine will die after it goes a few miles, or it will stall repeatedly. Change the filter with every tune-up, major or minor. Ask the mechanic to install the type that also fights vapor lock, a condition where heated gases prevent liquid gasoline from reaching the carburetor; these filters include a way to hook up a fuel-vapor return line into the filter.

If you suspect you took on a tankful of dirty gasoline cut with water by an unscrupulous seller, at least get the fuel filter changed. You may have to have the tank drained and the fuel lines blown out. Get suspicious if the car starts feeling anemic or stalls suddenly—and repeatedly. Never go to that station again. If you start using gasohol, get your fuel filter changed after two tankfuls. The alcohol in the gasohol cleans out the gas tank and gas lines and the filter traps all this crud.

The fuel filter is also one of the candidates for freeze-up when cold weather sets in; this is because it collects its share of water. Once the cold comes, we add a gas-line antifreeze to at least every other tankful. (DryGas, a trade name, has become almost generic for products of this nature. They contain methanol—or methyl alcohol, to be technical—an alternate fuel that attracts and helps neutralize water. Methanol is the fuel used in Indianapolis-type racing; it is not to be confused with ethanol, the extender ingredient in gasohol. Ethanol does not attract water, but it, like methanol, retards formation of gums in the engine.) Buy gas-line antifreeze for straight gasoline in bulk at discount stores. If you buy only at retail, you increase your cost up to 70 percent. Cars using gasohol usually need not worry about frozen pump or gas lines.

Transmission Filter | Did you know there was such a thing as a transmission filter? The majority of people, including car salesmen, don't.

This filter should be replaced whenever you inspect the automatic transmission or get a transmission tune-up. For city or heavy-duty driving (severe service), that should be every 15,000 to 20,000 miles. However, we know of a garage man who on his own new cars opens the transmission and cleans the filter after 10,000 miles. He claims that the transmission components grind off rough edges against one another, causing metal filings, and that the sand from casting the aluminum housings is most likely to be shaken out of remote crannies. Thus he reasons that cleaning this debris out after 10,000 miles insures trouble-free operation for years to come. After this first change he waits between 15,000 and 20,000 miles for another filter change.

The transmission filter can be made of paper, felt, or a mesh screen. General servicemen sometimes don't like to replace them because they think it is difficult and they know it is messy. We must confess that on some of the cars we owned we didn't bother to change the filter until double the mileage recommended above, and we suffered no ill effects. But a new factor is entering the picture. U.S. car makers are asking lighter transmissions to do multiple duty on different engines, changing only a few gears. They don't give the same overengineering that provided a safety margin for neglectful car owners. The later the model of car you own, the more important it is to follow at least the manufacturer's recommendations, even shortening them in many cases on transmission service.

Emissions Filters | Until now we have been discussing filters that protect the powertrain of your car. The positive crankcase ventilation (PCV) system and the vapor canister filter (if your car has one or both) protect the environment from your car's byproducts. Since they are monitoring and cleaning what the engine produces, they can affect efficiency of operation. Plugging off these emissions controls is not only illegal for the mechanic who does it for you but is also increasingly self-defeating. As car makers refine engine performance, they adjust the engine's components to mesh with emissions controls. If you plug off the controls, you had better be prepared to alter the engine to achieve the expected increase in fuel economy. Apart from the legality of the alteration, it is not cost-effective in most cases.

Find out if your car has a filter for the PCV system; it is something found on some later model cars that is supposed to filter the air being drawn into the crankcase. It is another filter that most people—including many mechanics—never heard of. It's located somewhere around the air filter. Change it about every 15,000 miles at the maximum or whenever you replace the PCV valve.

Finally, inside the vapor canister—the thing that looks like a black coffee can—there is a flat air filter, which is replaceable on the majority of U.S. cars. The vapor canister, located toward the front of the engine, traps gas vapors and distributes them into the combustion mixture. Replace the filter with every tune-up, even though it seldom if ever clogs. Ask about this one.

In summary, what Priority One and Priority Two do for your car is to protect its powertrain from premature or unnecessary wear and tear. When you do this, you have won more than half of the battle. When you do it *yourself*, you have gained in satisfaction and saved money, too.

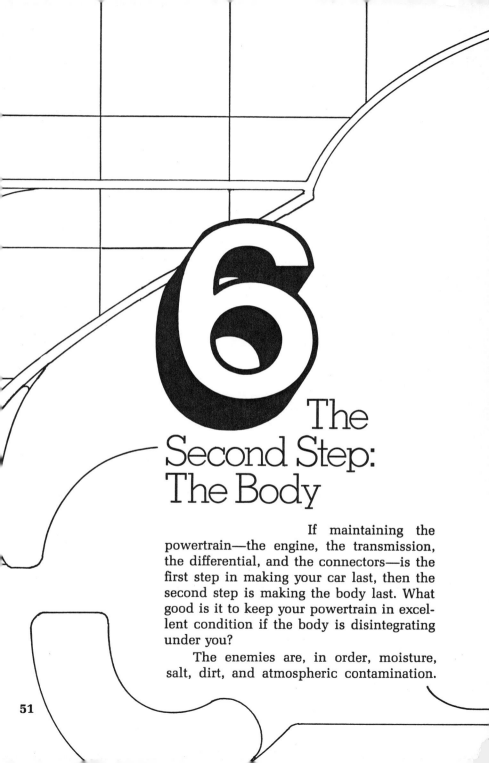

6

The Second Step: The Body

If maintaining the powertrain—the engine, the transmission, the differential, and the connectors—is the first step in making your car last, then the second step is making the body last. What good is it to keep your powertrain in excellent condition if the body is disintegrating under you?

The enemies are, in order, moisture, salt, dirt, and atmospheric contamination.

You can defeat them, but this is difficult in an older car, where they have already had a head start. Car makers have done a very uneven job of protecting their product from rust or corrosion. Although the U.S. companies are beginning to offer warranties against rust perforation, this means that the vehicle must have rusted through before you can collect. Surface rust, no matter how bad, doesn't count. So U.S. car makers are saying only that their car bodies and frames won't rust through. Since car bodies don't usually rust through in the 36 months allotted by the shortest of the warranties, the warranty covers only very unusual cases.

WHAT PROTECTION MANUFACTURERS PROVIDE

The maintenance of a car body that is still composed primarily of steel requires vigilance whether or not you rustproof. Let's back up and see what measures the car maker takes to make sure the vehicle will resist rust or corrosion. Not every car is given the same protection and, as noted, it is only since 1975 that anticorrosion measures have improved in U.S. cars. That may have been because thinner steel is now in general use. If unprotected, this steel obviously will rust through faster, since it's thinner. The Model A Ford in 1929 used 0.048-inch-thick steel for fenders. Up until the mid-1950s, 0.037 was the minimum, but with the advent of Vega and Pinto, the thickness dropped to 0.032—and this became general when weight became a dirty word in the industry. Some Toyotas contained 0.029-inch sheet metal as early as 1975. If you want a frame of reference, that is about three times the thickness of a steel beer can.

High-strength low-alloy steels add another factor. Although they tend to be used in slightly thicker gauges, they rust more quickly, since they are mostly ferrite and have very little alloy. Sheet steel contains both pearlite, which contains carbon and is stronger, and ferrite, which does not and is more formable. They are combined for their respective qualities, but under electrolytic action each corrodes or rusts.

Particularly when building a less-expensive car, car makers have not been noted for their antirust measures, which cost money. Witness the severe rust problems in early Pintos and Vegas—two years to perforation in fender areas in some environments. Witness the VW Beetle's corrosion under the battery box, or the tailgates on almost any pre-1975 wagon, or trunk floors, spare-tire wells, some front suspension parts, and even brake lines. These are not isolated cases. Pick the make, and like as not there's a rust horror story somewhere.

If your car has steel brake lines covered with terne, a combination of tin and lead, you should know that if a flying stone nicks this coating, you can have sudden serious problems. Salt spray can act as the electrical conductor between the tin in the terne and the steel. The line will then rust through very quickly. Since the brakes work under pressure, the leak can cause brake failure at any time.

There has been some retreat from unitized bodies specifically because of rust problems. Unitized bodies have no frame to take stress. They get strength from box sections (which have four sides like a box) made of thin sheet steel—very rust-prone. Frame-and-body construction tends to use thicker steel for the frame, which takes the stress. If the car maker sticks to recommended Society of Automotive Engineers (SAE) designs for various kind of joints, hat sections (a section that looks like a hat), electrical connections, box sections, and bolt connections, a vehicle made by frame-and-body construction should resist rust well beyond four years. Unfortunately, car makers don't always follow SAE recommendations, and unless you're a body engineer, you won't be able to tell.

The auto industry can stop rust for five years or more while using steel. It won't use the simplest rustproofing method, however, because you probably wouldn't stand for it. If you have a steel ashcan you can look at the solution —steel galvanized (coated with zinc) on both sides. In addition to protecting steel from rust, galvanizing does two key things to the metal—it makes it harder to form and harder to paint. So, while car manufacturers can make simple shapes for particularly corrosion-prone parts like rocker panels, valances, cross members, and frame rails, they hesitate to form fender outers, hoods, roofs, deck lids, and lower rear panels out of galvanized steel.

During manufacture, most car makers dip the body in a bath that protects the sheet steel and chassis. The protective coating, a step in the paint process, is basically a zinc-chromate solution, first cousin to galvanizing the metal. The bath, however, does not penetrate to all inside surfaces, such as headlight eyebrows and inner rails or door inners. Nor does it seal seams. Car makers use spray-on vinyl plastisols to seal seams, but these do nothing for inner surfaces in box and hat sections.

And that has permitted a whole outside rustproofing industry to arise. These rustproofers drill in and use special tools to coat these inside surfaces, and then insert plugs into the drill holes. The ultimate irony is that current American Motors cars are protected with a version of one of these outside processes.

Another current American practice is to add antirust paints to the lower third of the car in addition to everything else. Recently, a further step has been taken, a vinyl film applied just below the finish coats on the lower fenders and rocker-panel area. This film helps to defeat salt spray and will resist paint chipping from pebbles.

Rust can be prevented even on thinner metals. As we said, most cars now have some galvanized steel at corrosion-prone areas. Another antirust material used at these vulnerable points is Zincrometal, steel whose surface is covered at the foundry with a patented zinc-based primer. For instance, on some of the more expensive General Motors cars, the door outer is made of Zincrometal, which on the untreated side is painted with electrophoretic paint—paint that resists electrolysis. Then the assembled door has wax sprayed inside, with particular attention to the door bottom. All makers use this method inside hollows to some extent, but production-line speed can make this protection more theoretical than real. If the worker misses, it is expensive to redress his error later.

The ultimate move to defeat rust is by switching components to plastic. Plastics never rust, are unlikely to corrode, and save weight. Examples of plastics on your car are likely to be the front fender inners, the front panel under the bumper, and the panels housing the headlights and taillights. On some cars as early as 1974, there's a single piece for the headlight-grille area. Remember this for consideration when you're thinking of upgrading your present car, a subject we discuss later.

Another problem is electrochemical reaction, which occurs when aluminum or chrome-plated brightwork —molding, window trim, light surround—is imposed over steel. If there is no rubber or film interface, this reaction eventually can corrode the body metal and provide an easy mark for moisture. That's why interfaces are being placed under brightwork of any kind and why car makers have been switching to moldings that are bonded to the vehicles by adhesives. The other reason for switching to bonded moldings is elimination of holes from attachment devices. Every hole eliminated is one less place where moisture can infiltrate.

As more and better manufacturing techniques utilizing adhesives become cost-effective, car makers are expanding their uses. Adhesives are especially good where unlike materials are being joined, since the adhesive can be manufactured to compensate for the different rates of expansion of steel and aluminum alloy, for instance, or steel and polypropylene plastic.

Increasingly, in better-made cars, metal edges are never left raw, and thus prone to rust; they are turned and protected with film or other coatings. This care has nothing to do with price. You can find the evidence on the edges on the unnoticed side of the door near the hinge. Compare a 1973 Chevrolet with a Citation. Even more impressive is the finishing on the edges in an inexpensive vehicle like the Mazda GLC; compare that to luxury cars from other nations. This extra care in manufacturing is a measure of the value the manufacturer wishes to build into the vehicle. When you find such touches, you have discovered a vehicle that will be easier to keep a long time.

WHAT YOU CAN DO TO PROTECT YOUR CAR

The plain fact is that cars will eventually rust out if not protected and maintained. How do you protect your car? You should worry most about any metal crease, bend, or seam. These are the places on the car where moisture or salt solution can accumulate. When you ignore damage from a minor fender-bender, you are inviting the onset of rust and corrosion.

Rust can also accumulate in the edge of a wheel opening or in the rear door sill. We picked these examples for a reason. On the wheel-opening edge you can install a chrome or plastic trim that resists the moisture and salt spray. The rear door sill is not that simple, since the moisture gathers inside a closed section. You have no way of knowing if the dip process coated those inner surfaces.

But it still pays for you to fight the good fight, new car or car in use. For instance, while Ziebart—one of the oldest of the after-purchase rustproofers—insists the protection won't work except on a new vehicle. J. C. Penney applies its material to "twelve vulnerable areas" of any vehicle in reasonable condition. Penney's is cheaper, too. Tuff-Kote Dinol, another brand, also does used cars but reduces the limited warranty from five to two years.

Which of the after-manufacture antirust treatments do you choose? If you are considering a new car, you should shop the rust treatment more carefully than you choose accessories. There are many on the market—Tuff-Kote Dinol, Ziebart, Rusty Jones, Polyglycoat Rust Treatment, and Sym-Tech, among others.

All use a combination of rust inhibitors, resins, and waxes. All companies agree that these must be applied under pressure. Some companies say that you should drill to the tough areas and do the job in one step, while others claim that two steps are necessary. There is no rustproofing treatment we know that is for the do-it-yourselfer, so you'll need to have an independent franchise or a car dealer do the job.

Car dealers don't do older cars, where any treatment has to displace moisture and penetrate oily road film and existing rust as well as seal the surface against water and salt spray. Neither do many of the franchises. Most seek vehicles new or almost new. That alone will cut your search, as will the fact that some are sold only by car dealers and some only by independents.

Strangely, none of the car magazines, no government agency, and no one else to our knowledge has tested the various products impartially to see which is best. You should examine warranty length, compare where and how the material is applied, and find out who claims what before you buy or authorize rustproofing.

One final tip for owners of older cars who now want the protection. Invest in a steam cleaning of the underbody before applying rustproofing there, but make sure the surfaces have dried off.

Plain old ordinary creosote undercoating, once called an antirust coating, is really a sound-deadener. Everybody has an improved version that gives some protection by blocking out moisture and salt spray. If the undercoating cracks with age and abuse, however, the crack provides a safe haven for wet and salt, which corrodes the metal.

You need to decide whether the protection you get is worth the money charged, or whether you can go with a different antirust application for less money. The longest limited warranty on an antirust system is seven years at this writing, a bit longer if you count the booster treatment. But soon, keeping a car a long time is going to mean keeping it at least a decade. Since few antirust systems give booster shots except in special circumstances, additional body maintenance will be necessary.

That brings us to the second enemy, road salt, which is conquerable by good antirust procedures and good maintenance. The further north you are, the more salt the highway department dumps to keep the roads passable. During a particularly bad winter, so much road salt is used that adjoining groundwater can be contaminated.

Road salt is the greatest stimulus to the auto business ever devised in the name of safety and convenience. Whatever happened to roads covered with packed snow and the use of snow tires? Salt solutions eat away at some protectants, require special paints, and generally deteriorate the automobile by corroding steel and even weakening some plastic. The car splashes itself with salt during a season when it does not get cleaned for months. In every cranny where water goes, so does a salt solution deadlier than Cleopatra's asp. Freezing slush packs into the fender wells and holds wet salt against the underside, where it can do most damage if the metal is unprotected. Incidentally, dry salt residue is much less active than wet.

Fighting road salt is ultimately a matter of removing it. That means washing the car more often in the winter than you do in the summer. Unless you want to practice driving on glare ice, that is not easy to do in your own driveway. Thus, you must accept the expense of patronizing the local car wash. Even assuming a $4 charge, a weekly wash would cost you some $52 over a 13-week salt season—less than the seat covers you bought, and far more critical for vehicle longevity.

Should finding a car wash prove a problem, at least clean the packed snow out of the fender wells and garage your car. You might hand-wash at least the bottom third in the garage.

Incidentally, lest those in the semiarid Great Southwest feel too lucky, there is a local villain there, too. It's called alkali dust, and it also eats cars. You need the washing routine as much or more than those in the North. At least you will have no problem finding an open car wash in the winter, whereas many Northern washes close with the first snowflake.

These professional washes not only remove salt, but also remove dirt and possible discoloration. Car washes come in all degrees of sophistication, from stalls where you squirt water and detergent to those automated ones with, we understand, go-go girls to watch instead of your car. With all due respect to the entertainment, we feel that watching the car in this case is more important. You want a car wash that will first and foremost clean your car exterior thoroughly first time through. Particularly dirty cars should be sprayed with extra detergent around fenders, wheels, and rocker panels if the machine's brushes can't do this job. If you find a car wash that doesn't accomplish this, cross it off your list. After that, it is a case of how complete a job you desire. Many vacuum interiors and clean windows inside and out. A few make an extra effort with whitewalls. One even squirted a piny odor in the car.

Should you buy the wax treatment? Not if you are going to wax the car yourself. You can add another coat of wax any time the car is clean—or if you have succumbed to the siren song of polymeric coating at $150 or more from the dealer or $30 Starbrite from the five-and-dime, you can apply the booster treatment that both claim are necessary. The polymerics like Polyglycoat are rivaling the waxes in popularity these days.

Road salt and sulfur dioxide in the air can discolor light cars and dull darker hues. Let us understand our goals. We want to make the car "shine like new," protect the paint against tiny scratches that come from dust in the air, and seal the surface against moisture. The first reason is what most people care about; the others are more important to the life and appearance of the car. If you paid for Polyglycoat,

Zeegard, Ultraseal, or the like on your new car, that's some protection, if you follow their directions as to reapplications. If you don't, you're eventually behind even the guy who uses no wax or polish. We'll talk more about them later.

For most of us with cars from the pre-Polyglycoat era, the answer may be carnauba wax, with or without acrylic additives. Carnauba wax is special. It is derived from a tropical palm, and it protects well, is very durable and polishes to a high gloss. But car waxes and polishes are sold under myriad brand names, all of which make claims of various kinds. Let's try to categorize by type:

"Pure" wax protectants

Cleaner-waxes and liquids

"Pure" cleaners

Compounding polishes

Polymeric treatments

"Pure" wax protectants come in paste form and take effort to apply. Moreover, you should polish the vehicle first. All contain some softeners and solvents, so although they are not 100 percent "pure" wax, they are closer than liquid. A few even contain compounding elements and are classified with the "pure" waxes only because they have relatively more wax. The more softeners—for easier application—and other additives, the less wax per can. It's better to use a power buffer and a protectant containing more wax than to use a softer compound. Although you would be able to finish the job quicker, you would get less-durable protection from the softer stuff.

Cleaner-waxes save you steps. Ideally, after washing the vehicle, you should use a car cleaner-polish to prepare the surface for waxing. The cleaner-wax combines these steps. Petroleum solvents and a small amount of compound are mixed with waxes, a polymer (usually acrylic), and liquefiers so that you can clean, polish, and wax in one operation.

Sometimes the ingredients permit you to do the job in the sun; sometimes shade is required because the solvents evaporate too quickly otherwise. If you have washed thoroughly with a good car wash or had it done, these products can do a good job on newer or well-maintained older cars. The way we do it is to make it a two-stage project. About a week after the major effort, we hose the vehicle off, then apply more of the cleaner-wax. We believe we get longer protection—almost as good as a paste-wax job.

Compounding, a very fine abrasive that minimizes microscopic scratches, is present in most cleaner-waxes, as we said. You don't need it for maintenance use except where paint surfaces are weathered from neglect or where you want to rub out discoloration or a scratch that has not reached bare metal. It works by removing the top paint molecules. Thus, it needs to be used very carefully and very sparingly, according to directions on the can.

Maintaining the shine of a car is a task just about anyone with at least one arm and some desire can accomplish. It is a bit more difficult to bring a car finish back to mint condition, because there is no correction for surface damage, tiny scratches, and the dullness of weathering that have already occurred. In the latter case, it pays to have a professional buffing and Simonizing—unless you are prepared for a five- or six-hour job where you *will* be using compounding, where you must be meticulously accurate, and where you will also probably find myriad nicks that will defeat your effort to make the vehicle like new unless you are also prepared to use touch-up paint.

When you wax the car, think of the wax as a protective coating. Thus, finishing the broad exterior surfaces is only part of the job. First, make sure you get the door edges, the panel under the front bumper, the rocker panel, and the wheel-opening edge. Other places often neglected are door sills and the areas under hinges, the underside of the trunk lid before the rubber seal, the hood and trunk lid channels, the rain gutters, and the painted surfaces within the car. Make sure you polish and wax around the rear window, getting into the indentation between the body and the molding and around the door uppers. Clean out and wax the splice where the windshield wipers recess; this is a prime location for moisture.

If you use cleaner-waxes or easy-on paste waxes, count on waxing at least once a month. The wax should protect longer in most environments, but not much. You are erring on the side of caution if at all; you also will find the wax buildup makes reapplication even less of an effort.

If you paste-wax and buff, you may go two months between applications, depending upon the contaminants in the air. It is a measure of our times that many of us breathe air that can deteriorate the finish of a car. In any case, remember to wash the car before waxing, or you will be grinding dirt into the finish.

Polymeric coatings have become very popular, thanks to the brilliant marketing effort of the Polyglycoat Company. The polymer is supposed to fill between the molecules of paint, thus creating a new surface. They offer the car dealer an additional profit center, and they can be machine-buffed. Treated cars look sensational when the coating is new. We have already commented on the need to follow the manufacturer's recommendations with this product category. You can try it on older cars: there are several brands and, we suspect, several slightly different formulations; but follow directions carefully or you will waste your money.

After that, it's a matter of washing the car properly. If you wash the car by hand, you can contribute to the demise of the finish with poor washing procedure. The rules are simple.

1) Examine the vehicle before washing. Preclean any road tar or bug or bird residue with bug-and-tar cleaner. Doing this before washing precludes spot washing the affected surface afterward.

2) Always use a car-washing solution to surround and dislodge dirt, dust, grease, and salt. Whether you apply it by hand with a sponge or with a brush-and-rinse applicator attached to the hose, you need that detergent. Plain water and pressure will not do the job, particularly with the dust particles that cling by static electricity. Each particle is a microscopic diamond-hard cutting tool. If it is not dislodged, you will help it scratch the paint when you dry the car by hand. If you are not likely to buy car wash, use a laundry product. Dishwashing detergent seems to work quite well: you want a high-suds rather than a low-suds product. Do not use soap; it leaves a film.

3) Use quality sponges—real sponges work best but are sometimes hard to find—and rinse them often. Cover a section at a time with foam and hose it off. Work from top to bottom since, in case you hadn't noticed, water runs down the car, not up it.

4) If you really care about the vehicle, dry with chamois skin or the like only. It's quicker and more efficient. Toweling is the next choice, but it leaves lint, whether cloth or paper. A sponge is good if it is large enough, but don't use anything else.

If the car looks streaked after drying, you didn't wash it well or the detergent you used was ineffective. Either try something else and wash again or go to that car wash we mentioned earlier.

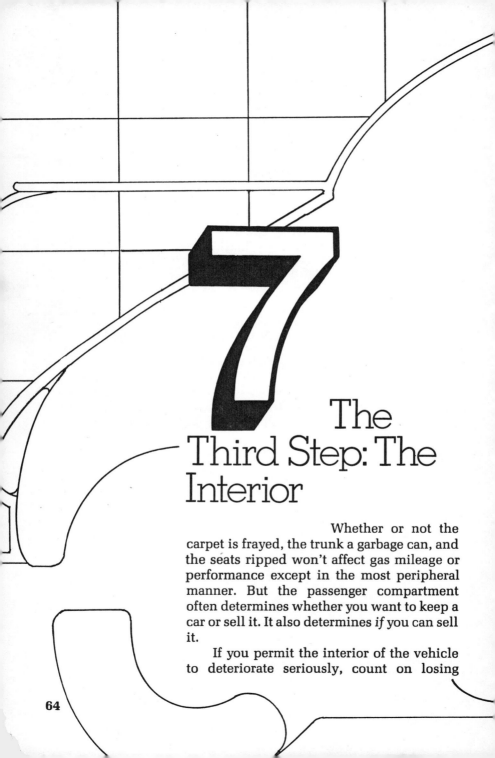

7

The Third Step: The Interior

Whether or not the carpet is frayed, the trunk a garbage can, and the seats ripped won't affect gas mileage or performance except in the most peripheral manner. But the passenger compartment often determines whether you want to keep a car or sell it. It also determines *if* you can sell it.

If you permit the interior of the vehicle to deteriorate seriously, count on losing anywhere from $200 on up if you try to dispose of it. Also—if you are honest about things—you know that you will feel less and less disposed to keep the vehicle yourself.

Care of the interior of a car is even simpler than caring for the exterior—*if* you clean it regularly. And if you begin before grit and gravel ruin the carpets and various stains ruin the upholstery, both carpet and upholstery should last a long time and look good doing it.

THE TOOLS OF THE JOB

The number-one tool for interior care is a vacuum cleaner. Many car washes feature coin-operated vacuums that are much more powerful than the home version. In fact, these vacuums will suck up your tie, your gloves, and any small change lost in the vehicle if you aren't careful. You should figure on vacuuming the car at least once a week. If the cost is 25¢, that's only $18 a year.

Another excellent vacuum is the wet-or-dry canister type, which can do almost as well as the best of the commercial units. If you have one of these, don't wait to remove the leavings of a particularly dusty, gravelly, or muddy trip—do it right after you come home.

Well down the line in effectiveness are the cigar-lighter plug-in types. They don't have much suction power but do have the convenience of portability. Your home vacuum is okay only if the dirt isn't drawn directly through the motor, as it is in most uprights. Ask the store that sold it to you. If the dirt is so drawn, you risk ruining that kind of vacuum cleaner with pebbles.

We mentioned weekly vacuuming. Try to do the trunk, too. Inspect trunk walls and floor for rust at the same time—weekly. It is only through a regular routine that you are going to keep this car spotless and in good repair as well as desirable.

Sooner or later you will be face to face with the question of how to clean the seats. No covering will survive a cigarette burn unscathed, and stains like blood, some soft drinks, and gum can still wreak havoc on most seats. The best defense is in methodical application of the next set of "tools"—various cleaning and protectant substances, water, rags, and toweling. Any one of a number of car shampoos for the dirt of general wear works on cloth and will usually handle blood, coffee, gum, or even soap scum.

It is ironic that the availability of more durable seat fabrics and vinyls has led to the general decline of cloth or woven seat covers. (Plastic see-through "breathable" covers still have a small but loyal clique.) The only seat cover that seems to be in a growth pattern is the sheepskin.

Vinyls are often preferred because of ease of maintenance. Most spills and stains wipe off with a damp—not wet—cloth. Vinyl seat covers with "breathable" perforations will not be bothered by water, but keep it to a minimum, because the excess will drip onto the carpet.

Vinyl or PVC (polyvinyl chloride) seats have two drawbacks. They retain heat in the summer and stay cold in the winter. In older cars and some foreign vehicles the PVC gives off an emission that lightly coats the insides of windows. Ever since our 1967 Volvo 144 proceeded to its next owner, we have preferred cloth or part-cloth seats. Recently, plastics engineers have claimed that better PVC formulation has either totally or largely eliminated the emission problem. White or light-colored vinyl trim or upholstery needs even closer care than dark brown, blue, green, or black upholstery. With enough work and cleaning, you can bring back the light vinyl in older cars to like-new condition. Then you should protect it with one of the general treatments.

Vinyl seats are slipperier, so winter clothing slides in and over them easier. Washable terry cloth covers, held in place with elastic straps, can be put on for the summer season. They are an excellent investment, especially if you go to salt-water beaches. Salt water is not supposed to hurt PVC, but if it soaks into the foam padding through a seam or rip, it creates an odor very difficult to get rid of.

The cloth currently used to upholster seats is far more

durable than most of what was used in the 1960s. Even velours and materials that look like crushed velvet are made from polyesters, nylons, and rayon blends. These stand up to wear and tear amazingly well. These innovations have caused the seat-cover business to deteriorate. Although there are plenty of seat coverings available, you don't automatically drive your new pride and joy into the local shop for protection that was all too necessary in the 1950s and 1960s. This is because many car makers Scotchgard the seating, using the same water- and stain-resistant protectant that goes on upholstered furniture. Recently car dealers have been merchandising a similar treatment for both vinyl and cloth seats. They offer to treat new cars and they claim to protect everything—the carpet, the vinyl door, dashboard and seat trim, the cloth seat fabric, as well as the headliner and rear shelf.

If you are willing to invest the time and do a careful job, you can buy similar materials and enjoy the knowledge that you saved money. There are any number of such protectants —including Scotchgard spray for the fabric and carpet. Some that come to mind—the power of positive advertising —are Armorall, Tag 14, Son-of-a-Gun, Westley's, Turtle Wax, and Lexol. Before applying in a less-than-new car, vacuum and clean until it looks like new. Then apply the protection. Be warned beforehand that Armorall and friends tend to give vinyls and leather a sheen. If you don't like that kind of sheen, don't use these products. The gloss never completely wears off—even though the treatment needs periodic booster applications.

GETTING THE JOB DONE

The way to attack the cleaning and protection of the interior is to begin at the top and work down and in. Clean and protect the headliner first. Unless you have unusual habits or badly behaved children, it is likely to be reasonably clean to the naked eye. Headliners range from vinylized fabric to foam-and-plastic one-piece versions. The reason for protecting them is to ward off dust and ultraviolet rays, ozone and atmospheric contaminants. The former bother some people; the latter promote fading and discoloration.

Then do the doors and quarter panels, the dashboard and firewall and console. Then come the seats, starting from the top. Remember to protect the backs of the front seats. Finally, work on the carpet.

We go into this obvious detailing of simple procedures because through experience with otherwise rational and intelligent people, we've found an almost pathological reluctance to do the drudgery of cleaning and protection in the methodical manner necessary. It's a case of "If you do it right the first time, the next time is easier." You must have the intelligence to realize that you are accomplishing something beneficial and conserving both your resources and those of the nation.

The necessity to be methodical about maintenance is a thread that runs through this entire book. The idea is to forestall wear, forestall problems, and even to forestall boredom by doing something before damage begins. And if you are methodical, you will find you spend less time than you would in disorganized efforts.

While you are cleaning and protecting, take the opportunity to inspect for loose or missing screws, wobbly handles, and tarnished interior chrome. This is the time to tighten or replace the screws, polish the chrome, and repair the handles.

It is also a time to lubricate manually operated seat mechanisms, to make sure emergency brakes operate properly, to reglue or replace moldings and the pads on the accelerator, brake, and clutch pedals, and to run a check on your dashboard warning lights. You may want to go back to the owner's manual and relearn the location of everything on the dash and below it: particularly where the fuse box is, if it is inside, and where the master switch is. If you are really brave, see if you can figure which wire goes where. Don't touch, just trace; they're color-coded, so it's fairly easy.

Cleaning "chrome"—often metalized plastic—is a key activity because it makes the car look newer quickly. You can use a special chrome cleaner, but any protectant has the ability to make these touches shine with a little extra wiping.

One warning: make sure you don't scratch the covers of the instrument dials. Use a clean, soft cloth or paper towel. These faces are scratchable plastic, usually acrylic.

A key operation—and our pet peeve—is keeping the insides of windows and the rear-view mirror clean. This has to do with safety. If your ability to see is impeded, you are less safe. This cleaning should be done as often as is necessary; in smaller cars driven by smokers, that could be every other day. You know film and fingerprints are clouding the windows if you can't see as clearly as though you were outside.

When cleaning windows, please use cloth towels, a specially treated cloth, or soft paper towels. Newspaper can be used *after* it is soaked. Then it gets soft enough. *Do not* rub with dry newspaper on dry glass.

Someone should invent a tool for cleaning the inside of windshields and rear windows. Squeegees are the wrong shape to get the corners and it's difficult to work around the rear-view mirror. For this job, one's wrists seem to be pointed in the wrong direction.

Water with ammonia is an excellent window washer. Any of the preparations with diatomaceous earth in the liquid are also fine, although more expensive. All do a good job, but you need at least some elbow grease.

ABOUT SEAT COVERS AND SEATS

You may think, "If I am going to keep this car as close to forever as possible, perhaps it *would* be better to cover the seats." Well, there are two schools of thought: one feels that you use the seats until they are worn, ripped, or too dirty to clean, and then you cover them. The other school thinks that you should put the covering on when new or nearly so, so that when the covering wears out, you can remove it and the car will look new again.

We can see the advantage of seat covers if they are well made and well fitted. There are two traditional semipermanent kinds obtainable commercially: the plastic see-through type and the kind made of a durable cloth (woven plastic-straw types, which deteriorate quickly, have become difficult to obtain, thank goodness). They are rarely sewn on; rather, they are fitted with metal or plastic clips. A good semipermanent seat cover should fit as well as the slipcovers on the living-room furniture. It will cost as much or more than good slipcovers and, frankly, we don't know why.

An alternative covering gaining popularity each year is sheepskin. Sheepskin is warm in the winter, absorbent in the summer and, if you get a dark color, it doesn't show dirt. It comes as a throw, as a cover attached by elastic straps, and as shaped and fitted seat covers. It comes with the wool left long and with the wool sheared, natural or dyed, and in various grades. Although many people buy sheepskin covers by mail, we believe it's much safer if you can see, touch, and feel the actual covers before purchase. Good sheepskin covers are supple (not stiff), have wool that is fleecy and thick, and attachments comparable to those on semipermanent seat covers. Moreover, they should last and last and last. We believe most people will be happier with the wool dyed to a medium or darker color rather than natural, which tends to be yellowish. If you have no experience with sheepskin, go down to an auto-accessory store and look the samples over before you make a final judgment on whether you want them.

Of late, a sort of compromise version has arisen. These cover the front of the seat back and are held in place with straps. They are less expensive. Good full covers of sheepskin can cost you as much as $450 if you have a large sedan. For that investment you should get durability and looks.

Another solution to the seat-cover problem is to cut

them and sew them yourself out of canvas, nylon, or some such durable material, or have them made by anyone who knows how to use a sewing machine. Making the pattern to cut the material is easy for anyone who makes clothes or has ever made a template. Just overcut a bit, so if you mismeasure, you'll have enough material when you fit.

Old curtains, if they are of a strong material, can have new life as seat covers. The pattern or color is a matter of your taste. Treat them with fabric protectant.

To keep seats in shape it's also important that there's enough padding to resist sag. This is a problem in so-called economy and compact cars and even in intermediates. It is less of a problem on the so-called full-size vehicles, but it is still a problem there.

Some people assume the seating isn't going to last for a good long life and so, when the car is new or nearly so, they add stuffing or have an upholsterer add stuffing. Others, the author included, prefer to wait until the first sign of seat sag, and then not only get the stuffing added but have the seat springs retied and any minor tears in the fabric repaired.

Later-model General Motors cars may have all-foam seats, which are supposed to last longer and are simpler in construction. However, a good auto upholsterer can add denser and firmer foam to improve support for the thighs, the lower lumbar region, and the shoulders.

Eventually you may want to consider substitute seating. Although most specialty seats are bought when the car is purchased or shortly thereafter by sports-car enthusiasts, the specialty bucket seats—Recaro, Scheel, Corbeau—could improve family sedans as well. Custom seats are only for front seating. If you have two seating positions in front and never use the front center seat, you can transform the car with custom seats and gain comfort and driving pleasure. However, like any product, these seats come in grades, sizes, and seat widths. The most expensive at this writing run $1,100 per seat; a $300 seat made by the same company is superior to most original equipment.

Since the main market for these seats is in sports and sporty cars and there is a feeling that all those drivers fit into French-cut jeans, seat cushions tend to be narrow. Make sure the seat cushion is wide enough to be comfortable. The seat should enclose you, supporting not only the thighs but the sides and back as well. All of these custom seats, of course, are shaped differently. Some are true bucket seats in the simplest meaning. Others are segmented to adjust every part of where you are in contact. Do you wish to go this route? Try to get a demo ride. The better ones should last far beyond original-equipment seating and you can transfer them from car to car.

PROTECTING AND RENEWING CARPETS

Finally, we're down to the bottom line—carpeting. I am told that carpeting is a relatively recent phenomenon, and that cars came through first with a bare floor, and then with rubber mats. Carpeting and the padding underneath serve a useful purpose: they act as sound barriers and insulation from heat or cold. For most, however, they are cosmetic, giving the passenger compartment a finished "living-room" look. No other part of the vehicle so blatantly distinguishes economy and luxury as the carpet and padding. Rubber is now reserved for trucks and off-road vehicles unless you deliberately rip out the carpeting. All the rest have some grade of woven carpet.

Carpet grade is expressed in the ounces that a unit weighs. If it's 10-ounce carpet, it means the unit of carpet weighs 10 ounces. If it's 20-ounce, then either the weaver has packed twice as many threads into the same unit or the carpet has heavier backing. Most economy-car carpet is woven to commercial grade with its threads tightly curled to resist dirt. However, since pile carpet looks much more luxurious, someone started using it in automobiles. Cut-pile carpet is now in more and more vehicles. It holds dirt and may hold stains, but feels better under your feet. You need to give it extra care, as previously described.

If the carpeting eventually wears out or if you decide to upgrade, there are custom kits available for many vehicles. You remove the old carpet, install the new, and that's it. Some of these kits, however, contain an even lighter grade of carpeting than your car started with. If you have a popular U.S. car of an older vintage, you may do better by ordering car factory carpeting from a more luxurious version of your model or from a sister vehicle. There is interchangeability among some Dodge, Plymouth, and Chrysler models, among Buick, Chevy, Olds, and Pontiac, and among Concord and AMC Hornet.

Get a price from an auto-upholstery shop for the job, too. You will have a greater selection of carpeting, and *they* will do the work.

An alternative is to leave the worn carpeting on and get fitted rugs. Since there's no need to do anything but drop the rugs atop the regular carpeting, your labor is minimal. And you have the advantage of being able to remove the rugs for really thorough cleaning.

The most common alternative is rubber mats. These come in various shapes and grades. Generally, the thicker the rubber, the better the grade. You must nevertheless maintain these mats to keep them looking new. This includes periodic hosing and washing. Keep an old toothbrush handy to get dirt out from the grooves and designs that are in most rubber mats. (The toothbrush cleans grooves on your pedals, too.) One warning: make sure the mats are dry on both sides before putting them back into the car.

Some people get rugs and then put small rubber mats atop them. That is overkill, but to each his own. Some cars have carpeting on the door kick plate: we think this is an excellent idea, because carpet resists scuffs with less visible wear. If you can match the carpet, have your doors so protected. It's an excellent upgrading device.

One final note on carpeting: very early in your ownership, pick up an edge of the carpet and examine the padding.

If there are white stains on it, you have a water-damaged vehicle. If it was represented to you as new, you have been ripped off, because it may have been in a flood where water penetrated the frame, etc., accelerating rust or affecting brakes and suspension. Talk to the person where you bought the car. If he will not help you, report it to the manufacturer and the local prosecutor.

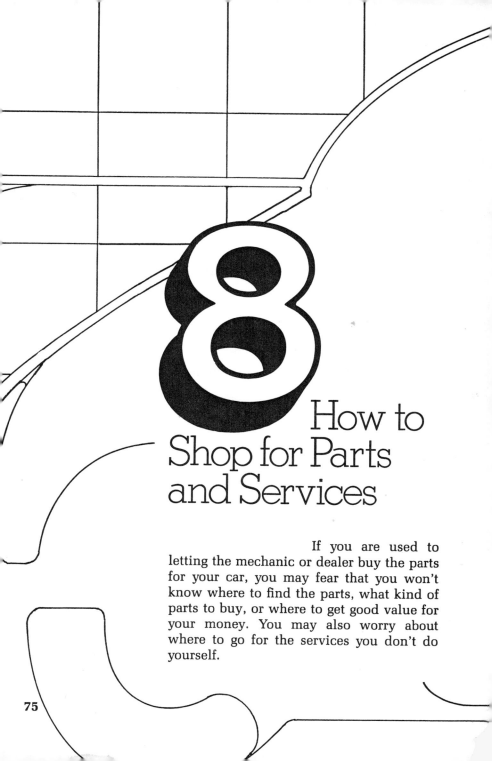

How to Shop for Parts and Services

If you are used to letting the mechanic or dealer buy the parts for your car, you may fear that you won't know where to find the parts, what kind of parts to buy, or where to get good value for your money. You may also worry about where to go for the services you don't do yourself.

SHOULD YOU BUY NEW OR USED PARTS?

The problem of getting good value on parts involves more than knowing where to buy any given part most inexpensively. It also involves knowing whether a rebuilding of your part, a remanufactured part, or a used part would stand you in good stead at less cost than a new part. Even if you have a job done at a garage or service station, you can tell the mechanic whether you are willing to use a rebuilt, a used, or a new part. If you are not certain of the pros and cons of the specific case but do want to save money, have the mechanic answer the following questions:

1) Can you obtain a rebuilt or used part instead of a new one?

2) What will the cost savings be?

3) Is there a major difference in how reliable and long-lasting the rebuilt or used part should be, compared to a new part?

For instance, a rebuilt or remanufactured carburetor may cost 40 percent less than a new one, and it should be just as reliable and durable. A used carburetor, properly cleaned and adjusted, may be an even better buy, assuming you can find one and assuming either you or an expert can certify its condition. Or maybe all that you need is a carburetor-rebuild kit in order for you or the mechanic to fix your old one.

Remanufactured electric fuel pumps and water pumps also save money over new pumps and yet they don't compromise reliability. Unless you are very knowledgeable, sometimes the service outlet may give you a rebuilt one and charge you for new, so you should communicate your desires beforehand.

There are over 15,000 parts in an automobile, we are told, but no one need be terrified by such a figure. Unless there is an accident, at least 10,000 of these will last the life of the vehicle. They include all sorts of fasteners, pieces of sheet metal, frame or unit-body components, interior hardware, and so forth. You will be concerned primarily with the powertrain, electrical system, wheels, steering, and suspension. And much of this subdivides into component systems that last and last when given proper maintenance. However, there are still enough left to make a multi-billion-dollar business for the aftermarket. Part of this is in replacement parts, part is in accessories, part has to do with appearance, and part is the maintenance items.

Briefly, here are some of the key components besides carburetors and water pumps that may present you with a choice. (We also won't mention engine blocks, because no one we know has ever bought one new.)

Fuel Pumps | It usually pays to buy new *vacuum* fuel pumps, but

rebuilts are generally available. If the rebuilding is local, you are taking a risk if you don't know who rebuilt it. If it is remanufactured by a major firm, you can be a bit more certain it will have a new diaphragm pump arm and check valves. Remanufactured *electric* fuel pumps save more money, and so make more sense. If you can do the rebuilding yourself, you can buy your own rebuild kit for either type.

Transmissions | Few automatic transmissions need to be replaced

totally. An entirely new transmission would be prohibitively expensive. What you get at a transmission shop if you need it is a rebuild. Ask the transmission man if he would install a used unit if you can find one at a wrecker. Usually each engine fits onto more than one automatic transmission. So you can update, save money, and get a guarantee from the wrecker in the bargain. However, if you need to replace a manual transmission (total breakdowns are even rarer), you will find few transmission shops qualified. The junkyard will have few of these; so buy new gears, etc., for a rebuild at the dealer's or a qualified garage.

Electrical Components | Hardly anyone buys new alternators, voltage regulators, or starter motors. There are excellent rebuilts from national companies. Try updating your electrical system when parts fail if you can get good advice on what parts to substitute. However, if you can't, or don't wish to use rebuilts, the answer is to buy small items like voltage regulators and distributor caps new. Windshield-wiper motors can be bought new or used. Spark plugs should always be new. Use the correct plug of a given brand for your engine and kind of driving. Consult the spark-plug maker's equivalency chart if you are changing from the brand recommended in your owner's manual.

Batteries | We are firm believers in using a battery that is more powerful than the one specified by the car manufacturer. While you can get excellent replacement batteries from junkyards and they can last for years, still we will go for a new maintenance-free 70-amp-hour replacement for a four-cylinder car, even though it may cost six times as much. We want the luxury of knowing that the car will start anytime, any weather, anywhere. Most manufacturers, however, say 40 to 45 amp hours would be good enough for such a car, even with air conditioning. Look in your owner's manual for the maker's recommendation and then get a more powerful one.

Tires | Recaps cost less than new tires, but vary widely in quality and durability. Prices for new tires are so heavily marked up that you can almost always get a discount, even on premium radials. If you are trying to keep your car for the longest time possible, we believe that using retreads and tires that give less mileage and poorer efficiency does not make sense. The exception is the radial snow tire, which is used only part time. Here, factors other than price are primary. Junkyards seldom have used top-drawer radials.

WHERE TO SHOP | Where do you shop for parts?

Can you save money on a part by shopping knowledgeably? It's self-evident that making a car last and last becomes more rewarding if you know that you are accomplishing the goal at the lowest possible cost and with little or no loss in reliability. Throughout this book we've indicated some stratagems to accomplish this. For instance, on crash parts (parts likely to be damaged in a crash), your junk dealer or wrecker is your best alternate source. He also may be the prime source for used engine and transmission parts, and for replacement seats. Following is a list of where else you can buy parts and supplies. Ideally, you would have enough time to shop around until you found absolute best buys, but nowadays neither the time nor the cost of driving permits this course of action. Once you have some idea of what to expect at each source, you can save yourself both time and cost by telephoning beforehand.

Supermarkets | Many food markets have items like oil, anti-

freeze-coolant, filters, cleaners, wiper blades, and even spark plugs on a few shelves. These are regarded as convenience items for the food shopper who may also be changing his car's oil. Prices tend to be competitive or higher, very seldom lower. Selection is of course usually limited.

Discount Stores | Many discount stores have separate auto de-

partments. They offer the items supermarkets carry, but in greater selection, as well as other relatively fast-moving items like floor mats, chains, mirrors, touch-up paint, wheel covers, tune-up kits, oil-change kits, etc. Discount rate and variety of inventory vary from store to store. Usually, there's very little discount from the prices in supermarkets and department stores. The advantages are convenience, the ability to use your credit card, and usually a liberal return policy.

Department Stores | Some department stores have auto departments inside the store. Others, in particular J. C. Penney, Sears, Montgomery Ward, and some smaller chains, have separate auto parts and service centers. The latter tend to be more complete in relatively fast-moving parts, and sell tires and perhaps mufflers, too. The former—disappearing fast —specialize in the same material that discount stores have. Incidentally, some discount stores (K-Mart in some places) also have service and repair centers. All accept credit cards.

Auto Specialty and Speed Shops | Often the widest selection of fast-moving generalized auto-related items is found in these stores. You need to spend some time at a good specialty or speed shop to get some idea of the scope of gadgetry and accessories available for your car. Another major advantage of this kind of store is the knowledge on servicing and parts that you can pick up by asking questions of the personnel. Prices are generally no lower than department stores. Store personnel also may know of specialist mechanics and painters to help you improve your car.

Mail-Order Houses | These establishments range from the likes of Sears and Montgomery Ward to oil companies to auto-specialty houses, and they vary widely in the variety of merchandise ordered and in speed of delivery. You can get bargains if you know how to read catalogues. These catalogues also give you an idea of what a given part or accessory costs in a store, as for instance the Sears catalogue regularly beats the price for the same item in the Sears retail store. The main advantage to shopping in a store is immediate acquisition. You still can shop, however, by comparing like items in different catalogues or with a store. To get a fair comparison between a store price and a mail-order price, always remember to add the cost of freight and tax, if any, to the mail-order item. Write away for catalogues from Sears, Montgomery Ward, and auto specialty places, whose names you can find in any auto-enthusiast magazine.

Jobbers **|** The jobber is one of the middlemen in the auto-parts distribution chain. Jobbers are listed in the Yellow Pages. Some have stores, which may sell to other stores and mechanics and also to savvy members of the general public. While you will not get the same price as a store or even the professional mechanic would, you should get a better price here than in a retail establishment. You need to know exactly what you want and have some idea of its price. Ask for discounts if you can pass for a pro. Usually, these places can supply you with everything but crash parts.

Service Stations and Garages **|** Unless the part is on special sale—like tires or batteries—this is strictly retail buying. If you are getting a repair done, even on something like a battery replacement, the garage will take a markup on the parts required. That's because a garage probably doesn't buy enough either from the local car dealer or the jobber to merit deep discounts. That may not be true with garages that specialize in a particular make. If you wish to save money on a major repair, tell the mechanic right off the bat that you may want to buy any major parts for him. For minor parts like plugs and points, you won't save enough to bother. Parts specific to a given model are going to be purchased either at the wrecker or at the car dealer. Whether you want to shop or let him shop is up to you, but at least inquire what source he will use.

Car Dealers **|** The myth of the superiority of original-equipment parts is one of the most pernicious in the auto-repair industry. The car dealer has a virtual monopoly on all sorts of specific components and new sheet metal. He does not have a monopoly on brakes, shock absorbers, exhaust systems, carburetors, or even engine blocks. Often the after-market component is superior to *and* less expensive than original equipment. Sometimes it's so far superior that it's worth it for the caring car owner to pay more—as, for instance, with shock absorbers.

Many car dealers who run good parts departments and seek retail parts customers will carry some items not stamped Mopar, Motorcraft, Delco, etc., the original equipment brands. Check this out. Parts men at car dealers who want to cultivate retail trade will give you suggestions on what is superior if they carry more than one item. You don't need to buy there. However, they are the main source if you are updating appearance or moving parts and need to know what fits what.

Other Possibilities

Two come immediately to mind: discount buyer services fostered by, say, a credit union or the AAA, and tire stores. The former should be checked out for tires, batteries, and some accessories. They sell above jobber prices, below retail. In addition to wheels and tires, tire stores almost always carry fast-moving accessories. They also make simple repairs—alignment and tire-related services, as well as usually brake jobs, muffler work, and simple tune-ups. By all means investigate buyer services if they have what you want! Tire stores may save you a little when you buy their brand of battery, etc., but otherwise they are on a par with auto specialty shops in price.

Before you have any need to buy anything specific, investigate all sources and get some idea of relative prices and what each source carries. Then, when you need to buy something, you can zero in on the right place.

PAYING TO GET IT DONE

Buying labor is a bit more difficult. There are five general categories besides the car dealer where you can get work done. They are the service station, the garage, the mass merchandiser, the specialty shop, and the body shop. If you don't know your car, as advocated elsewhere in this book, you are at the mercy of the mechanic or service writer (the person in the dealership who listens to what's wrong and writes it up). You don't know whether you are being overcharged, or ripped off by unnecessary repairs or shoddy work. Yet any or all of these categories may contain knowledgeable, ethical individuals. We believe that throughout the service industry, it's lack of proper training and tools that leads to most shoddy or unsatisfactory work. The problem is compounded by customers who are ignorant of how a car works and who have unrealistic expectations of what they should receive for a given expenditure as well as by service people unable or unwilling to take the time at the beginning to explain what to expect.

Car Dealer I On paper it looks as though the dealer's service department should have the overwhelming advantage: the car dealer must have the proper tools for a given make, he is encouraged to have the proper diagnostic equipment, and his men must attend schools sponsored by the car maker for specialty training. A franchised dealer is also obligated to make repairs under warranty and extended protection plans. In addition, he has the added incentive of hoping you will buy or lease a car from him. Unfortunately, a few dealers consider the service department a necessary evil and run it inefficiently. Modern car dealers are notorious for their ignorance of how a car works, because the vast majority of the dealers rose from sales, not service. Or if your car is the orphan line in a multi-line dealership, the dealer has the minimum possible servicemen for your car.

How can you tell? There are several ways. See what the service area looks like. Is it reasonably clean? Does it have diagnostic equipment (boxes that roll around, with dials on the face and wires that are attached to the car)? Does it have other specialized equipment? Ask how many NIASE (National Institute for Auto Service Excellence) certified men are in the shop, and how many men have certificates from the manufacturer. Dealers are proud of this accreditation. Either way, you pay for the advantages of having your car repaired at a dealer. Dealer service at retail costs $30 or more an hour in some locales. At those rates, you have a right to excellence. If you are dissatisfied with the dealer from whom you bought the car and you have good reports on another nearby dealer, switch while the car is still under warranty.

However, after the warranty is finished, you may feel constrained to try to find less costly service for some routine jobs. The dealer, some body shops, and some specialty shops work out of flat-rate books provided either by trade publishers like Chilton and Motor or by their manufacturer. These tell them the average time that a particular operation should take. That's what they usually charge, no matter what the actual time is (unless it takes appreciably longer). What you seek is a charge either at real time or at a lower retail rate. What you also seek is equal-quality work. Below are the alternative possibilities.

Service Stations | These are usually good for light repairs, major tune-ups if they have an oscilloscope, and minor tune-ups otherwise. They can do light repairs on the order of changing tires or wipers, some carburetor work, or replacing fuses and switches. Some also specialize in transmission or brakes beyond the light repairs. It's good to have a service-station repairman you trust, especially if he's the type who will diagnose ills that he doesn't wish to touch and send you elsewhere for these.

General Garages | They do light repairs and tune-ups, and may do front-end work, brake service, exhaust-system service, transmission work. They may also align wheels. Look here too for NIASE certification in some specialty. (NIASE certification is not general: it is for a specific specialty like brakes or air conditioning.)

General garages run the gamut of competence and expertise. Many specialize in a given make or in imports or some part of the car. The only way to find out how good any recommended place is to go in and have work done there. After all, you are seeking competence and not creative genius. Get an estimate beforehand, as at your car dealer, and make sure to formally authorize any work. No pigs in a poke; let him know what he's supposed to do beforehand, even if it's in general terms. Most garages use the flat-rate manuals but charge a lower hourly rate than the dealer.

Mass Merchandisers |

These do the volume repairs, tune-ups, brakes, exhaust systems, and alignment. They include stores like Sears, J. C. Penney, Firestone, and Goodyear. Watch for specials in the papers and don't be afraid to take your car back until they do it right. Help at these places tends to be transient, since when the people learn the job well, they can make more money elsewhere. Usually there are a few key personnel: you get lucky if they do your job.

Specialty Shops |

In a search for greater profits, your Superior Muffler man is doing much more these days than exhaust systems. Your Midas Muffler man does brake jobs. And your local brake shop may do wheel alignment and mufflers. In other words, while these people in franchise stores may specialize in one thing, the scope of their services is closer to that of a general garage, tire store, or mass merchandiser.

This weakens the rationale that a specialist—since he is doing one thing all the time—will be the expert and will be able to do it cheaper because he stocks only the necessary parts in volume and can work quicker. We would still consider Superior Muffler or Midas or Aamco or whatever for their specialties, but we would price them out. Even the dealer is cheaper sometimes.

There are other specialty shops that really are specialty shops—your local radiator place, your spring and suspension shop, and local transmission or brake stores. These places may cater to commercial accounts, but if you have what is obviously a radiator problem, why let the garage take it down and charge you a markup? Why not take it down yourself?

Body Shops |

An accident is the most likely reason you will not be able to keep a car for a very long time. That's why body shops are so important. Body shops are somewhat like mortuaries: the average person is forced into contact at a time of stress and emergency, and he has no idea of fair prices nor is he thinking clearly or logically. This often results in one of two courses of action: the owner of the damaged car accepts the repair place recommended by the insurance company or he lets the car dealer handle it, figuring that the insurance company will bear the added cost, if any. One is like being Little Red Riding Hood asking the wolf if he eats meat, and the other is like fumbling the ball away on your own two-yard line and expecting the opposition not to score. Obviously, the insurance company is going to pay out as little money as possible on your claim.

Insurance-company profits are affected directly by the amount of money they pay out to repair or write off vehicles. They are not really interested in whether the repair is well done. More and more, they try to pay only to bring the car to its previous condition. In other words, if you drive a 1978 model and the rear quarter panel has been severely scratched, they will paint only the rear quarter panel even if it means that there is a discernible color difference between it and contiguous sheet metal, a difference that diminishes the value of the car. Some companies will fight you on rerustproofing and undercoating components and will not pay for a new part if wear can be presumed. We're telling you this only to drive away the idea that an accident will be a painless way to make your 1978 automobile like new. And we're telling you this to make sure you inform the insurance company before any mishaps if you wish to have them replace an exotic paint job or added equipment. There are arguments either way. If you tell them, they may try to raise your premium. If you don't, they probably won't pay extra.

In partial defense of the insurance companies, they give you a list of places to choose from where they know a repair can be done within the price allowed. These places *will* perform as to price on repairs authorized or get axed from the list. What you need to worry about is whether the company is allowing for *all* damage and for a *high-quality* repair. That is why you should get a second opinion from some shop not on the approved list before accepting the insurance-company offer. We prefer to pay the local dealer—especially if he has a body shop, and most especially if an import or luxury vehicle is involved. You can be positive the local dealer will specify new crash parts more readily than he will recommend straightening and filling. Some people think they must accept whatever the insurance company offers. That is not so. You have the recourse of demanding arbitration or, in an extreme case, of suing.

However, if you chose to go to the dealer first and the cost of repair is coming mainly out of your own hide, also get a second opinion from another body shop before authorizing repair.

One of the advantages of repainting for updating is that you get to shop body shops for price and quality *before* any emergency and thus you already have gotten some idea of what you will receive for your repair dollar when an accident occurs. Ideally you will have found someone who will perform well when you have that emergency, although it is more likely you will only have a contact from whom you can get an estimate for a job at a predictable quality level.

There is one way to beat the system—sometimes. Let's say this is a damaged fender on a popular model of a popular make. You either have purchased a parts car or you know a wrecker who has the fender. Make the best insurance settlement you can, and then supply the body shop with the requisite parts. Depending upon the labor time allowed, you may have a chance to come out ahead. But cost out all the elements *before* you go this route.

In summation, experience is the only real way you will learn the intricacies of buying parts and services. Some people thrive on this aspect of auto ownership, and no matter where they live will find sources and procedures. They are the fortunate ones—not distracted by sports on TV or a friendly card game or the corner brewhouse. Although most of us will make the effort only when we need to, the important thing is to know that there is more than one way to keep the car attractive and running at minimum cost.

9

Troubleshooting Logically

It is entirely possible that, despite your best maintenance efforts, your vehicle may refuse to perform its function. If your efforts have been regular and thorough, the chances of this are very slim. But the car is a machine, and machines have problems sometimes. Until onboard diagnostics are more fully developed, you may miss a warning sign or a negligent mechanic may miss it for you.

We are lucky that we live in an era when computers are invading the automobile. In the future, we may face vehicles that are totally computer-controlled, if not computer-driven. But for the present, most of us need to worry about the cars we own now. We'll discuss later the onboard computers that diagnose troubles and are available for you to put in. For now, let's stick to two basics:

> What to do to pick up warning signs of impending trouble.

> How to diagnose woes without panicking and without feeling like some prehistoric creature plunked down suddenly into the twentieth century and its technology.

You have five working senses. If, for example, you see that a tire is flatter than its mates, you logically must assume something must be done to make it as round as its mates, and to do this you must find out and correct the reason it became flatter.

You therefore approach the tire and examine it more closely. You do not hear the hiss of air escaping, so you conclude that the leak, if there is one, is either very small or is plugged. You then touch the tire's tread carefully to see if a nail or a sharp object has intruded. If this checks out negative and the tire isn't too low, you drive to the nearest place with an air pump. When you try to add air, you hear the faint hiss of a leak in addition to the sound of air going in under pressure.

You have begun to isolate the problem and do something about it. The next thing you do is tell the service attendant what you have found, which will tell him that the tire is not holding air. If he is experienced, he will probably remove the wheel and tire, immerse the tire in a tub of water, and rotate it and look for bubbles on its surface. Or he may conclude you have a failing air valve. Then you get the repair made.

The example illustrates a process. Based on your senses, you should make decisions and take action. If you raise your car's hood and smell an acrid odor and, sniffing closer, isolate it to the wiring, logically you should get quickly to the nearest expert help—before you have the fire. Or if you see wisps of smoke coming from under the hood, you should pull over to the side of the road, turn off the engine, and get everyone out of the car. You know something is wrong. You also know that fires need air to grow, so you *don't* immediately open the hood. You let it sit. Is it a fire or a radiator boilover? Start sniffing. Wait and see if the smoke abates, listen if you hear the boiling of liquid or smell the acrid odor of singed wiring harness.

What we are trying to illustrate is that logic and some knowledge can keep you in control. It is logical that you must take action if you see a frayed wire, feel a soft radiator hose, or find fan-belt tension loosening. Either seek aid, replace the part yourself, or repair. For instance, you would tighten the fan belt to recommended tension. If we remain logical and methodical about the car, emergency situations will not arise out on the road, and the vehicle will operate to specification. But if we perceive the beginning of a problem and put off action, we are neither logical nor methodical, and the machine smites us.

Ignition | Let's illustrate the process of deduction one more time with the ultimate problem: the car won't start.

You get into the vehicle, turn the key, pump the accelerator, and nothing happens. You do it again—still no sound at all. Begin the process of elimination. Let's say you turned the key to ON and there was no sound at all. You know how cars start. The most important component is the battery. If the battery is low or dead, it cannot crank the engine. Ergo, you must test it. Turn on the dome light and watch it while you turn the key. If battery and starter motor are OK, the light will dim only momentarily.

It passed the test and you still can't start. Now open the hood and check to see how well the battery cables are attached. Are the terminals and clamps clean? Are they tight? If all this checks out, then you must suspect the starter motor and its connections. Locate it and check them. Sometimes the problem is only a loose connection.

Now let's assume you turn the key and instead of dead silence you hear a click. Then nothing happens. Obviously electricity is reaching out from the battery but something is not letting it get to where it can do its job. The most likely culprit is the starter motor, which can be either jammed or defective. If you have a shift car, you may be able to unjam it by shifting to second, turning off the ignition, and rocking the car until another click is heard. You *can't* do this with automatics: the starter must be freed in those cars by removing it.

What if you hear the starter motor cranking but the engine still won't start? Is it a rainy or snowy day? Has the vehicle been standing in the wet? The most common cause is damp ignition wires, spark plugs, or both. This prevents the voltage from reaching the plug tip where it produces the spark that fires the engine. If you're not out in the driving rain or snow, open the hood and check if the wires leading from the distributor to the plugs are moist or dirty. You can wipe them with a clean, dry rag, but it's better to use a special spray that is made to dry these parts. In a real pinch, dry the wires by wiping the wires and plugs with cigarette-lighter fluid, and pour a few drops of fluid over the distributor cap. *Do not smoke while you do this if you value your life!*

If you smell gas and the engine cranks but won't start, you have flooded the engine (that is, raw gas has gotten into places it shouldn't be, preventing ignition). Press the gas pedal to the floor and, holding it there, crank the starter continuously. The instant the engine attempts to start, release the gas pedal enough to keep it running. If this doesn't work within a minute or after two tries, don't waste the battery. You need to check elsewhere.

What you are doing in each case is making a diagnosis and, based on your knowledge of how the starting system works, trying to prove or disprove your theory by eliminating factors.

There are innumerable ways to use this process of

elimination elsewhere in the vehicle. And if you become expert enough to diagnose strange noises and sights and smells beforehand, you will be on your way toward making the car last without these various emergencies. In each of the following sections, we'll mention the key components and show what you can infer from physical evidence.

Tires **|** By "reading" the tread, you can find out about over- or underinflation, about unequal tire pressures, or about faulty wheel alignment. You can determine that your driving style requires a different kind of tire, or you can find out about loose suspension components or even a bent car frame.

If you look at the tread of your two front tires and see that one side is wearing differently from the other, you know that something is wrong. The easiest thing is to bring it in for the mechanic to diagnose. The second easiest is to check the air pressure in all four tires to make sure it is equal, and then bring the car in, knowing that the problem is not unequal pressure. Unequal tire pressure may also show up as a swerve to one direction, as vibration, or as a skid when braking.

The more curious or more aggressive will investigate further. The exact nature of the wear will give clues to the particular cause. For instance, one tire worn more heavily on the outside edge most likely means that the steering needs adjustment. In fact, several of these wear patterns can then cause the steering components to wear. Here are some other tire-wear patterns that indicate problems.

- If all tires are worn on both edges, but the tread in the middle is still in good condition, it means that the tire is underinflated (or that you drive too hard).

- If tires on one side of the car only are worn to the outside, it usually means that you have a misalignment or the frame is bent. It's a sign of excessive camber (which means that the wheel and tire are leaning out too much).

- If a tire is wearing on the outside edge but is forming a scalloped edge, this is called cupping. Check to see if the wheel is out of balance; if the ball joint is worn; or if the shock absorber has begun to fail.

- Feel to see if the tread is forming regular longitudinal ridges, which is called feathering. This is caused by misalignment, which usually comes on when you have hit a pothole or a curb particularly hard. The blow to the tire—which in a car with soft suspension may have seemed slight to you—threw the toe-in or toe-out off, and the tire now is scrubbing against the road surface erratically, like the wheels of a pull toy.

- If the middle of the tread pattern is wearing down quicker than the edges, the tire is overinflated.

You should replace the tire at once if you see the tread worn to the level of the wear bars that have been built into all tires since 1968. According to the National Tire Council, smooth or balding tires have 44 times more flats and are more than twice as likely to skid.

You should replace the tire at once if you discover a bump or bulge in the tread or sidewall. That means you probably damaged the tire internally, and tread or sidewall separation might cause a blowout any time. When you hit a curb or pothole hard enough, the tire can suffer internal damage. If you think you did this, have the tire in question examined as soon as possible. Driving on such a defect could render the tire useless. Tires flex 544 times every minute at 55 mph, one tire company claims, so you can imagine how quickly a defect can be exacerbated.

And you should replace any tire with a cut or crack deep enough to expose tire cords. Incidentally, when you inspect tread, remove stones, glass, or other debris. You never know when road, curb, or other pressure will drive that debris further into the tread and cause big trouble.

So tires can be clues to alignment, wheel balance, suspension wear, and your own driving shortcomings. Just learn to "read."

Under the Hood | In the paragraphs diagnosing starting woes, we mentioned some of the things you examined to figure out the source of the woes. We would wager that many of those components were telegraphing trouble well beforehand. If you look over the engine compartment carefully you'll get the telegram.

If either the battery tray or the terminals have a powdery white substance on them, you not only should clean it up, but you should examine the battery for defects and loose connections, and you should have the alternator and voltage regulator checked. If you don't have a maintenance-free battery, install one when the time comes for replacement. A maintenance-free battery has nowhere to add water.

If you look at the engine block or around the valve covers and see wet or oily spots, investigate. Depending upon location, wet spots can mean a faulty carburetor, a gasket problem, a seal giving out, or a sloppy installation of oil or automatic transmission fluid. Ask questions, even after the mechanic says what he thinks it is. You learn best when something's actually happening to you. For instance, if your car is three or more years old, the head gasket may be of a type that gets compressed after a time and then leaks minute amounts. You may need to tighten the cylinder-head bolts.

You may need to retorque all the bolts you see on the motor—intake and exhaust manifold, too. Loose bolts on the intake manifold may let air into the air fuel mix, and so cause difficult starting or stalling. Retorquing to specified tightness is a simple remedy that should be tried before you agree to more expensive and time-consuming work.

You can also adjust valves for wear in many engines. If you adjust annually, then you can often avoid paying for a major tune-up.

If you look at the radiator and there are dead bugs or other debris on the corrugated core, clean it off. If the core has a dent in the pattern the size of your thumbnail, check with an expert to make sure that flow hasn't been restricted.

One of the best reasons for changing or at least draining

your antifreeze-coolant twice a year instead of once every year or two is to ascertain what the internal condition of the radiator is, as well as preventing rust buildup. If you had expected to reinstall the old coolant, don't if it is rust-stained. Rusty coolant should make you consider doing two additional things: a reverse flush of the system—the water is forced into the system and sucked out—and adding a can of compatible antirust cooling-system conditioner.

Many cars come through with a coolant-recovery system. This system is helpful and very simple: nothing more than a plastic tank that catches coolant overflow; it's translucent, so you can easily see if you have enough coolant. You can top off your coolant through this reservoir without opening the pressure cap on the radiator. Usually you need to replace a few ounces a month, lost through evaporation. If your car doesn't have a coolant-recovery system, get one installed at the local radiator shop. It's relatively inexpensive and worth it to be able to know precisely how much coolant you have.

If you notice the needle on the temperature gauge moving more and more toward HOT, investigate logically. First, check the coolant level. The next most likely culprit is a weakening pressure cap. Have it tested and replace it if it is at all damaged, because as you know, without the boost in boiling point the pressure cap affords, a modern car is in big trouble.

A pressure cap's function is to raise the boiling point of the fluid in the radiator (cooling system) so that this fluid can transfer more heat from the motor. If the pressure inside the radiator is above one atmosphere (approximately 15 pounds per square inch), the boiling point must rise. Boilover occurs from a leaky pressure cap or temperatures so hot that the liquid's boiling point is achieved anyway.

Higher atmospheric pressures are in vogue, since most recent cars run hot. This is another good reason for coolant bottles, because if you open the pressure cap itself and something is awry, the super-heated fluid and possibly steam may erupt like Mount St. Helens and scald you.

Brakes | Sometimes brakes deteriorate so gradually that you—as the daily pilot—fail to notice. You can check pedal height for one clue as to brake condition. Another place to check is the wheels. If you see "oil" stains on the wheel hubs, that's cause enough to take it to an expert. Your wheel cylinders may be leaking, which will get progressively worse until the cylinder fails, and with it the system. As you know, brake fluid is non-compressible, and it seeks any escape when pushed against the components actuating a brake. When a leak occurs, it's like breaking the point off a pencil and then trying to write.

Transmission | Unfortunately, there are many cars on the road whose transmissions are only barely rugged enough for the size of the car. These are the direct result of U.S. companies striving to meet the corporate average fuel economy requirements of the government. Some accountant types in Detroit okayed the idea of building large, heavy cars with very small engines and a matching transmission. This powertrain had been excellent in the intermediate or compact, but when faced with the duty of overcoming the inertia and weight of the big car proved very marginal, to be charitable. If you are the owner of one of these 1977, 1978, or 1979 vehicles, you need to be extra sensitive to signs of transmission woes.

For instance, if the car jerks when you shift into DRIVE, LOW, REVERSE, or PARK, get a diagnosis. Now it may merely need a minor adjustment, but it could be worse later. If you feel or hear the engine whirring and there is no "pickup," get help. On some cars from the early to middle 1970s, the shift mechanism that reads P N D L R goes out of synch with use. Take the car back to the dealer and ask him to refer to service bulletins on the subject when making the repair. There are special parts substitutions.

An automatic transmission wastes gas by its very nature; that's the price you pay for the convenience. But you need not waste extra gas through malfunctions. Some people with acute hearing can hear the transmission shifting itself. This sound is normal. What is abnormal is when the car itself jerks.

With a shift car, you should never permit the clutch pedal to get to the point where it hits the floorboards upon contact, and you should start checking when shifting into or out of any gear becomes difficult.

Underneath | Without shock absorbers—properly called dampers by the British—there would be no control over the rebound action of the springs after driving over an irregularity in the road. They also control motions from side to side. The standard test is to stand on the bumper and exert pressure, and then jump off. If the car won't bounce at all, the shock absorbers probably have frozen stiff or a spring is broken; if the car looks like a pogo stick, the shocks have failed. The car should go up and down twice at most.

Springs themselves are subject to rust. They can loosen, they can tighten and wear from lack of lubrication, or they can weaken or break. Look at the car—see if it sags to one side. Other signs of trouble are ride deterioration (a harsher ride than you expect) and unexplained noises from underneath.

The kingpins in older cars (pre-1960) are the hinge-bolts for the front wheels. When they wear, the wheels tend to sag in at the top. Ride deterioration and tire wear from wheel shimmy are symptoms of trouble. If the steering wheel vibrates, check the kingpins. To check them, put the car on a lift or jack the front wheels up. Try to shake the wheel from the top. There should be no looseness at all. If there is, inspect the kingpins and wheel bearings. Newer cars have ball joints. They wear, too, and you can do the same checks for them.

Wheel bearings should be repacked with grease annually, in any case. When you check the kingpins, check the bearings. Hold the wheel on its sides and pull and push it. Listen for a whooshing sound or a sucking noise. If you hear it, the bearings may be loose. Try spinning the wheel by hand. No rotation? Either the bearings or the brakes (if they're drum-type) are too tight. This means that you are wasting gas again, in overcoming the friction.

Front-end alignment involves the kingpins or ball joints and the rods that tie the front wheels together. Hard steering (unfortunately often masked by power steering) and excessive tire wear are symptoms. This is a job for experts. Check it at least annually.

Wheels are often neglected. If each wheel is not reasonably round and balanced with the tire in place, you wear tires, waste gas, and ruin ride quality. Usually the wheels are in good shape and well balanced when the car is new, but contacts with curbs, potholes, and minor accidents may take their toll. If such occurrences seem to be severe, check the wheel to see if it is bent. Jack the wheel up and place a brick on the ground in front of the wheel. Now rotate the wheel slowly, noting the space between the brick and the wheel. It should remain constant.

Steering is most easily checked by moving the steering wheel back and forth while the car is at rest. If there is excessive motion, have the steering box adjusted and the steering components underneath checked.

While you have the car on the lift, check for oil stains or wetness on the underbody. If you see anything, get a satisfactory explanation. Remember, such stains should not be there. Period.

You will find that most troubles are likely to be involved with an electrical system. This is likely to change in the next several years as we move into more advanced automobile electronics. It is said that these systems will be available for many older cars as an update. Watch for the innovation, but cost it out before spending your money. We will discuss updating later.

Troubleshooting is an activity that anyone not overawed by automobiles can attempt. You need not do the actual repairs, but you do need to know what repairs are necessary. Experience in troubleshooting will help you make your car last and last. Try.

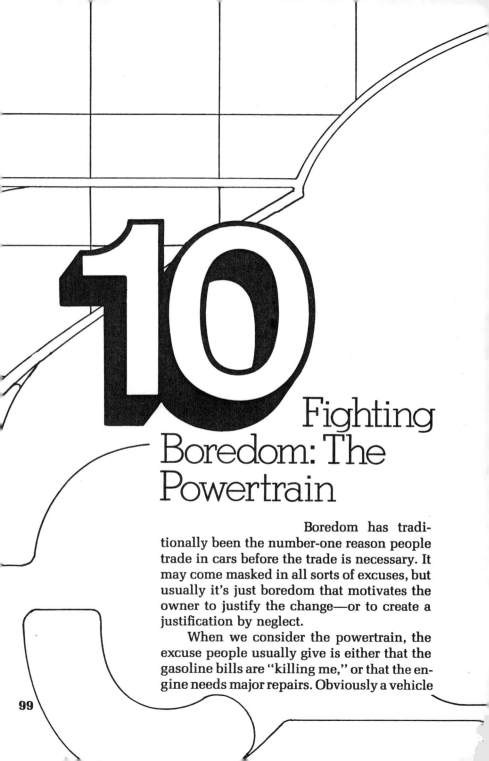

10
Fighting Boredom: The Powertrain

Boredom has traditionally been the number-one reason people trade in cars before the trade is necessary. It may come masked in all sorts of excuses, but usually it's just boredom that motivates the owner to justify the change—or to create a justification by neglect.

When we consider the powertrain, the excuse people usually give is either that the gasoline bills are "killing me," or that the engine needs major repairs. Obviously a vehicle that gets 15 real miles per gallon is less desirable than one that can get 23 to 24 mpg. By real miles per gallon we mean what you get with your kind of driving—not a laboratory EPA number or an advertised highway-mileage figure that is so phony it must carry an immediate disclaimer. But this is no reason to get rid of the car if it is otherwise acceptable.

Another excuse is range. With the fluid situation in fuel availability, it is certainly more convenient to go 500 miles between trips to the gas station rather than 300. But if this is the only problem, it makes a poor excuse and is easily overcome.

If you own this particular car primarily for transport, you should consider thinking about the car differently. The engine is replaceable, components of the engine are replaceable, the entire powertrain is replaceable—and the replacements can be better or entirely different. You are amortizing any changes over a long, long period, so the only limits are your ability to pay and your inclination or disinclination for innovation. But anything you do must be planned carefully beforehand; there's no reason to waste money.

Before anything else, however, you should inventory your powertrain's condition. Sometimes upgrading merely means getting the powertrain into the shape it was never in before, even when it was new.

For instance, on a conventional piston engine, first get a compression test or take it yourself with a relatively inexpensive compression tester. If there is a cylinder that tests out low, find out why from your expert auto mechanic. If all cylinders read low, you may need new rings. Returning the engine to proper compression is a major step toward fuel economy and efficiency. Sometimes, although not often, a leaking head gasket can cause low compression. Aftermarket sources swear that gasketing materials are continually being improved. If your motor block is messy, particularly at the joint of the intake manifold, you may find it worthwhile to consider replacing the head gasket. One warning: caution the mechanic to tighten the head bolts to the manufacturer's exact recommendation with a torque wrench; too tight is just as bad as too loose. There are cases where it would be beneficial for you to have the head (intake manifold) machined as well as the surface of the block. Extra machining can increase compression ratio slightly, and certainly brings the motor closer to design ratio.

The best way to receive a full picture on the engine's condition is to have it oscilloscoped. Many service stations and garages and most dealers own oscilloscopes of varying sophistication. The increased sophistication could make the task quicker and more accurate if the operator is competent.

There used to be many diagnostic centers that gave you a computer printout on what ailed your car and then priced the repairs. We always felt these were useful, so if one has survived in your area, check it out.

As powertrains are made less adjustable and more computerized, only oscilloscopes and such will diagnose car problems quickly. You may even have a diagnostic machine built into your vehicle.

Nevertheless, you may still check engine timing with a simple timing light and alter this to specifications.

Your strategy must begin on paper. The method is simple. List procedures logically and ask yourself and experts what benefit you can expect from each kind of upgrading. (We are presuming you have maintained the vehicle near design efficiency, a very bold assumption.) We have avoided exact cost figures, because they vary so much across the country. Here is a sample of what you might do.

Goals | Maximum engine efficiency, maximum fuel economy, avoidance of deterioration in legal performance.

Possibilities

Fuel-delivery changes

    1) Rework carburetor.

    2) Replace carburetor.

    3) Rework intake manifold.

4) Replace intake manifold.

5) Substitute electric fuel pump.

Fuel-combustion changes

1) Alter timing.

2) Alter spark intensity.

3) Alter air-fuel ratio.

4) Add water-vapor or alcohol injector.

Fuel-exhaust changes

1) Alter exhaust manifold.

2) Add turbocharger.

3) Alter exhaust system.

Fuel-emissions change

1) Add three-way or dual bed catalyst.

Transmission changes

1) Switch to five-speed manual.

2) Switch to four-speed automatic.

3) "Tune" automatic.

Radical alternatives

1) Change engine to more efficient one.

2) Switch to diesel.

3) Update entire powertrain.

4) Adapt for pure alcohol, dual fuel, or hybrid.

Other alternatives

1) Try synthetic oils.

2) Try special lubricators.

You now have enumerated possibilities that range in cost from a few dollars to as much as $5,000. Think carefully about what you seek to accomplish and how much you can afford. Before you commit yourself to a plan of action, have some idea of the end result and its cost. If you're set on contributing heavy interest to our financial institutions by trading in your car regularly, just do the minimum maintenance. If not, you probably need to upgrade.

Let's say you have a car you consider handsome, comfortable, and just about ideal except for its fuel appetite. You think you are prepared to use this vehicle forever and you have the money to invest in what then would become your ideal transportation unit. You are ready for a radical alternative and would be smart to consider converting to a true diesel, not the dieselized gas engines that General Motors and Volkswagen are peddling. Why? Because the true diesel—a Mercedes, Perkins, or Nissan, for instance—is much more ruggedly built and will last longer. While you are at it you should investigate switching to Ford's automatic-overdrive transmission to achieve the ultimate cruising mileage from this engine. For good measure you could see if you can turbocharge the diesel for better acceleration.

This is a project to dispel boredom and cash in large amounts. Assume, for example, that the vehicle is a 1979 Dodge van with a customized interior. You find yourself a firm like Vehicle Technology, Inc., in Queens, New York, which has been doing diesel conversions for the taxi industry, for American Motors Corporation, and for the Post Office; there are other firms with less-illustrious customers and maybe lower prices in other parts of the country. They will recommend a particular Nissan, Mitsubishi, or Perkins diesel, find out for you if the automatic overdrive matches, figure what has to be custom-made to connect the two, and fit the overdrive into the van. They could pick out a turbocharger, too. (Garrett AiResearch made one for the Nissan in International Harvester's Scout.)

You usually are given a ballpark figure for components, labor, and the time needed to make the conversion. If you are shrewd enough and use new engine and components, you may be able to get the job done for about $5,000. If you are talented enough to do it yourself, the cost could be half of that. If you can find and have a suitable used diesel rebuilt, the price goes down again. We recommend that you read *How to Convert Your Car, Van, or Pickup to Diesel* by Paul Dempsey.

Certainly there are less-ambitious plans that may be entirely satisfactory. Let's look at our list.

Fuel-Delivery Changes |

At this writing, it is possible to remove that gas-thirsty four-throat carburetor for a little over $150 and install a two-barrel job that will be more economical with minimal loss of legal performance. If you have a two-barrel carburetor already and still crave more economy, or if you just want to tone down your Quadrajet, you can usually install smaller jets or restrict the venturi. (Don't overdo this. You don't want to "starve" the engine. Have someone who works with carburetors advise you on how far you can go.)

Any U.S. car line has a number of optional engine families. Sometimes the difference is the carburetor and intake manifold. See if you can downsize into economy.

You can try converting to fuel injection, either the expensive cylinder fuel injection, as on Mercedes, or the manifold injection now in some 1981 cars. The latter is virtually a version of a carburetor, and the conversion should be both simpler and less exotic than cylinder systems, which will probably require a new or radically altered intake manifold. We recommend an electric fuel pump for any altered system, not because it will save fuel per se, but because fuel delivery is more precise with an electric pump than with a vacuum pump.

When you investigate some of the above alterations in fuel delivery, you may find that you need to alter wiring and electrical components. You may even be able to meet emissions requirements without the dreaded air pump. Find out beforehand; we know from experience how little some allegedly professional mechanics know about such matters.

Fuel-Combustion Changes | Most 1970s cars were set to run

rich (use more fuel in the fuel-air mixture) in order to meet
emission-control standards with the technology of the times.
You may remember Chrysler Corporation's "lean burn"
engines, which were considered technologically advanced
because they ran on lean mixtures. Your priority is to get
more miles from the fuel you burn, and that means that you
want to alter the fuel-combustion process. You are limited by
the design of the engine in the vehicle and the components.
Ideally, you burn a lean fuel-air mixture and burn it with
such intensity that there is little left to exhaust. This ideal is
never reached, but in the light of current knowledge a
well-read technician can use his electronic aids (oscilloscopes and engine analyzers) to find optimum timing, etc.,
for the components you decide upon. Remember, you have a
wide choice of spark plugs and heat ranges to aid you in this
search. Let's say you have mounted a two-barrel carburetor
to your V-8 via an adapter plate and also employ water
injection of some sort. Through trial and error, the good
technician can find the optimum plugs for these components—and it shouldn't take much error.

Fuel-Emissions Change | The lone legal fuel-emissions change

that seems to make sense if you seek economy is to free the
engine of earlier emissions systems by installing a three-way
catalyst system. By updating your emission control, you
should rid yourself of the power-robbing air pump. Stick to
the three-way system of your marque—the Ford system for
Ford cars, etc.

Fuel-Exhaust Changes | Dual exhaust systems will add to

engine efficiency by reducing back pressure. So will some
low-restriction mufflers—which might fail noise regulations, however. We have added a dual exhaust but, except for
the masculine rumbling exhaust tone, have observed no
change in efficiency at city driving speeds.

    Turbochargers, however, are another thing. What a

105

turbocharger does is to use the velocity of the exhaust flow to boost engine power during acceleration. The following is an oversimplification, but it's like a marathoner taking on carbohydrates to give himself extra go power. Boost pressure for street driving usually is very limited (6.5 pounds and under), but you can gain enough extra power to permit a smaller-displacement engine to approximate the acceleration of a normally aspirated larger engine. The fuel economy comes primarily in using the smaller engine. Turbochargers, however, exact their toll on engine innards. For instance, unless the valves are able to withstand the sudden rise in heat during boost, they may fail eventually. You should find out what your engine's innards are made of before dropping reasonably large money for an after-market turbocharger unit. In coming years there will be more and more original-equipment turbo installations, so you may wish to wait a year or two before making this change. Meanwhile, read up on it. Get brochures and other literature on the units on the market.

Transmission Changes |

Transmissions can be tuned, gear ratios may be altered, and final drives may be modified. Again, it's the kind of endeavor where you need an expert. For instance, if General Motors gains a mile or more per gallon by lengthening the final drive ratio from 3.50:1 to 2.46:1, you can too. (See Appendix One for an explanation of how the final drive works.) However, there are transmission wizards who do what General Motors doesn't: "tune" the gear ratios toward performance, economy, or a better compromise. If you have a torque-convertor automatic, they can play with the convertor for optimum efficiency.

It does not pay to install a lockup transmission instead of the conventional unless you are replacing the whole powertrain anyway. As for switching from automatic to four- or five-speed manual, this is another change hard to justify for most U.S. cars. It is expensive and time-consuming, even if the parts are available.

Radical Alternatives | Actually, switching engines or all running gear was not very radical at all twenty-five years ago. Now, however, one hears less about it because many engine switchers forget about reconnecting emissions equipment. Well, reconnecting is not that bad, and you can improve fuel economy when you swap engines. We have referred already to the diesel with its great durability and fuel miserliness. One can use other alternative engines, too.

The easiest is to pull out the big V-8 and opt for either a smaller V-8, a V-6, or a straight six-cylinder engine. If you have a 5,000-pound vehicle, use some judgment. Don't expect a Chevette engine to move it. But you can go from a 450 cid (cubic inch displacement) V-8 to a 305 cid V-8. Or if your engine is a 351 cid V-8, a 258 cid straight-six may do the job with the right carburetor-transmission-final-drive setup. Of course, "performance" will drop. You won't be able to accelerate as quickly, nor will you reach 55 mph quite as fast from a standing start—nor will you be able to reach more than twice the legal speed limit.

If you use the vehicle to tow a trailer, we believe you had best not change. Try getting better mileage other ways—by using 35 psi (pounds per square inch) pressures in your radial tires, by changing your driving style, or by streamlining the vehicle.

Any vehicle from 1977 intermediate-size on down can be changed by switching to a rotary engine or Wankel from a Mazda. There are two sizes, the 70 cid and the 80 cid. The latter—which was in the RX-4 series—is preferable for most U.S. cars. Try to find an engine from 1976 or later; in 1976 the rotary was reengineered for better economy. There are specialty shops all over the U.S. that can advise you on a case-by-case basis. You should gain smoothness (lack of engine vibration), cruising performance, and some fuel economy. You can gain even more fuel efficiency by fitting electronic ignition (as in the 1980 and later RX-7) or by swapping the thermal-reactor pollution system either for Mazda's 1981 catalytic-muffler version or for one of your expert's own devising. The latter course of action is likely to be only for those willing to break new ground. The payback will come in comfort and the knowledge that you own an absolutely unique vehicle.

Another whole class of radical solutions is in making your powertrain more directly controlled. For instance, you can convert the automatic choke your vehicle probably has to manual operation. Inexpensive conversion kits permit you to control the carburetor choke valve from the dashboard. The automatic mechanism thereby eliminated is one of the great gas wasters, because it is likely to keep the choke open longer than necessary during cold-engine start. If you control choking manually, you can push in the choke lever much sooner. Cold engines gulp gas. Hand throttles are also available to control idle speed.

Install an electric fuel pump or, for slightly less money, a pressure regulator for the vacuum-operated pump. The idea is to meter fuel flow. These are much less costly than the process of conversion to the electronic systems on some 1981 models.

Install cruise control if your car does not have it already and you do a fair amount of superhighway driving. You set the desired speed and the control—some under $50 installed at this writing—will hold that speed more efficiently than any human we've ever heard of.

For most of the time we have been aware of cars, water-vapor injection has been offered to improve performance and economy. The latest versions inject water and alcohol, which do help in cold starts. The units provide a water-methanol mist that is drawn with extra air into the intake manifold. This is said to increase volatility of the air-fuel mixture and promote more even burning. It works, but do you get enough of an mpg increase to justify the expense? Watch for this, although you may feel that mpg increase is an absolute must at any price. If you do install such a unit and use methanol in it, don't use gasohol. Or you can utilize only water injection to permit you to run older high-compression engines on today's lower octane fuel. On any water injection system the key is to meter the water and atomize it properly. At this writing EPA had certified only one system, made by the Goodman System, Armonk, New York.

You can buy a timing selector to advance or retard distributor spark from the dashboard, according to engine load or driving conditions. We insert this note, not because the selector is recommended, but because we believe that most drivers are not going to be able to select ideal distributor timing on the road and thus may be worse off than they are with the present compromise. The newest cars will do this electronically.

If the car doesn't have a flex fan or a thermostatic fan, you can purchase a flex fan. This fan changes the pitch of its blades as the vehicle gains speed and so reduces the drag on the engine. Finally, we can profit from a technique straight out of racing, if the car maker hasn't beaten us to it. We can force cooler, denser, outside air directly into the carburetor air cleaner to cure the possible air-starvation of the engine that can occur at higher speeds. The forward movement of the car forces the air through an air duct, through ducts opening behind the grille, or in the air dam below the bumper.

Please, please remember that the entire effort to fight boredom in the powertrain or anywhere else rests on your realization that the car is not an indivisible unit but can be improved or altered in part. This realization frees you from the trade-in cycle and permits rational use of your transportation dollar.

Other Alternatives | You may own a vehicle that will benefit from special lubricants or additives. The synthetic oils have been discussed previously; there are other formulations of non-petroleum materials beside the well-known Mobil 1, but we must confess no extended experience with them. Some, we are told, contain castor oil, which used to be put into racing engines.

We have more experience with oil additives, and for our cars, a 1973 V-8 (396 cid), a four-cylinder, and a rotary, we personally have had good luck so far with a PTFE called Tufoil. We followed directions explicitly and have observed better cold starts and mileage improvement varying with the vehicle.

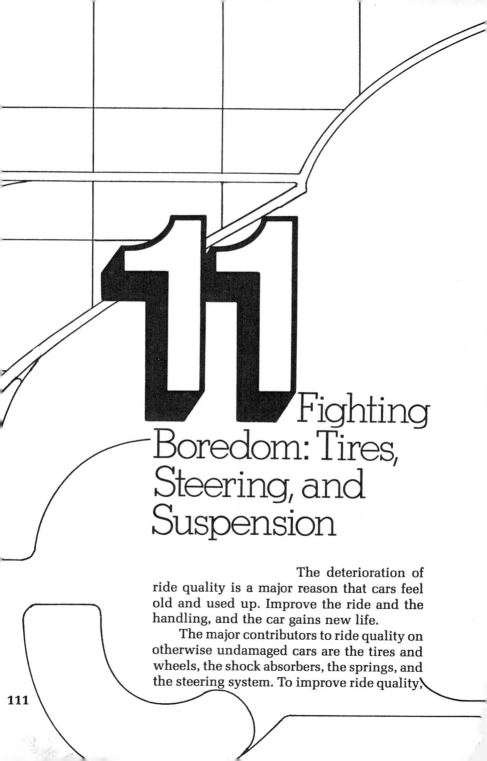

11

Fighting Boredom: Tires, Steering, and Suspension

The deterioration of ride quality is a major reason that cars feel old and used up. Improve the ride and the handling, and the car gains new life.

The major contributors to ride quality on otherwise undamaged cars are the tires and wheels, the shock absorbers, the springs, and the steering system. To improve ride quality, improve the parts in roughly that order. Usually you will need to work on most of these parts to achieve "design ride" or better. Since "design ride" on many U.S. sedans is so soft that a marshmallow seems like a rock in comparison, you may wish something safer, more efficient, and therefore better. Car companies recognize that one person's "living-room ride" is another's recipe for nausea; thus, you may find factory parts with which to upgrade. However, the after-market is full of equipment.

About Tires | We mention tires first because they are the most versatile elements and afford the least "technical" way to change ride quality. Adding or subtracting air costs nothing (most places), and the ride can be made harder or softer. Warning: Never run tires at pressures lower than those recommended by the car maker. Never run them above the limit on the sidewall of the tire. When you run tires with less air you lower the car's load capacity. More air, up to load limit, means more load capacity.

Without replacement, tires also may affect ride quality if they are out of round, if the wheel-tire combination is not balanced, or if the tread pattern is particularly aggressive, as on mud tires and snow tires. Seriously out-of-round tires sometimes can be corrected by shaving the tread. (When you see sales of "blems," often the blemish is evidence that the tire failed on roundness. It may be fine in other ways, but if you buy, you should be prepared for this possibility.)

Tire pressure can make a large difference. Try this experiment. When the tires are cold, put in 28 psi all around. Evaluate the ride and handling. Next morning put in 34 psi and evaluate this pressure, not only for ride quality but for maneuverability and, if you are going on a trip, for fuel economy. If 34 psi is not for you, try cutting pressure to 32 on a subsequent morning. It may be the proper compromise.

Tire pressure up front also can be utilized to alleviate understeer in rear-drive vehicles, particularly many sedans and coupes. By putting more air in the two front tires than the rear, say 34 front and 28 rear, you accomplish this. However, unless you are prepared for a unique tire-wear pattern, we believe this is a temporary measure.

There is another caveat. Tires vary not only in tread patterns and construction (see Appendix One) but also in hardness. A hard compound is likely to wear longer but give a harsher ride; it may deteriorate ride quality if pressures are too high, whereas the same pressure in a medium or soft compound might be perfectly acceptable. There is no longer any question that at legal speeds, radial construction tires are preferable in every case. But there is a wide variety of construction even among radials. The pattern in which the plies of reinforcing cord are laid on and the thickness of the cord strands both affect ride. The various reinforcing cords —steel, aramid fiber (Flexten), polyester, or nylon—also impart differing qualities. The manmade fibers give softer rides than steel, but may not last as long nor afford quite the same maneuverability. However, especially for older cars, the increased ride comfort is preferable to many.

Radials are also made in different heights and widths and with different profiles. Americans have been led to believe that wide tires with a low profile (ratio of height to width) are preferable, when it really depends upon the car and your goals. Generally speaking, wide tires have a larger footprint (the amount of rubber in contact with the road) and, therefore, more rolling resistance. That may be good for safety but it is not so good for fuel economy. Tires that are too wide for the vehicle may create so much rolling resistance that the engine may need to work extra hard to get them around corners and up hills and inclines. This wastes still more fuel and erodes rather than aids performance. It is interesting to note that the new high-pressure metric tire on many newer U.S. cars has a smaller footprint.

Tread pattern also affects ride quality, yet most people never bother to look at it. A very aggressive tread pattern like a mud and snow tire (wide separations) will be noisy, rough, and deteriorate ride on dry surface. It is designed to bite into snow or mud, but into nothing else. Examine the tread pattern. If it is the all-weather type currently in vogue, it should have ridges as well as a diagonal crosscut with angles called sipes. These sipes help stop water buildup and also interrupt heat buildup within the tire.

The whole subject of tires is fascinating if you are technically inclined. If you are not, just remember that the manufacturer's recommended size is a good compromise. If you switch from an 80-series tire (in which the tire height is 80 percent of its width) to a lower, wider 70 or even 50 or 60 series, you are increasing the amount of rubber on the road. This can improve ride comfort and it can affect handling and performance either way, depending upon other factors. It is likely to decrease fuel economy, and more likely to do so in smaller vehicles.

About Wheels | The general public usually forgets the wheel as a factor in ride quality. The clue to its importance is that Michelin, which makes some of the best tires, specified the exact manufacture of the wheel on its TRX wheel-tire combination, which is available in this country on some Ford Motor Company products. The design of the wheel permits the design of the tire to perform far better than it would on stock steel wheels. Part of the advantage is the reduction in unsprung weight; the other part is roundness. Unsprung weight is easy to figure out; it is weight not cushioned by the car's suspension (its springs and shock absorbers). It can have a tremendous effect on ride quality. Eliminating excess unsprung weight is one rationale for lightweight custom wheels (aluminum or so-called mag wheels). The other rationale is that lightweight wheels are rounder because they are custom made. This may be true where the wheel is truly custom made, but it is not necessarily always the case, and unfortunately it is not easy to check roundness before purchase. A reputable custom-wheel firm will replace a wheel that is far out of round, but in the less clear cases—where the degree of roundness is that of a steel disc wheel—you are unlikely to get much more than advice on how best to balance it.

Custom wheels generally are bought mainly for their appearance; the ride benefit is secondary. Just remember that complicated designs like starbursts are difficult to clean. Choose something rugged and simple, and learn *beforehand* any special directions on tire mounting, balancing, and possible air loss.

And then there are wheel covers that have no redeeming social value, are subject to damage and theft, and get dirty. The only possible rationale for some wheel covers is that they may improve the aerodynamics of the wheel. That is debatable for fake wire wheels and some other wind-catching designs. It is possible to manufacture a wheel "cover" that improves brake cooling, but you can't buy it for a passenger car. Wheel covers add unsprung weight. If you want better looks, save up and buy either the car maker's custom aluminum wheel or an after-market product. For the person retaining a vehicle for many years, it's likely to be less expensive.

About Shock Absorbers

Another area where ride can be transformed is in the damper or shock absorber. On a conventional car, there are four, one for each wheel; their purpose is to control bounce, rebound, and side sway. A jack-in-the-box demonstrates how the shock absorber controls motion. Jack's head is attached to a spring that permits it to wobble back and forth and up and down once it pops from the box. A shock absorber would control the wobble.

Since shock absorbers deteriorate slowly, ride quality and safety disappear while the regular driver accommodates himself to the change. However, when shocks are replaced, the improvement is so dramatic that the car feels renewed.

If there was only one change that we could afford on a car, we would spend the money on the best shock absorbers we could buy. With any luck, we would have enough to purchase something better than the original equipment. On most passenger sedans and coupes, original equipment shocks are marginal and not very durable. This is changing, but slowly. There are any number of premium and so-called heavy-duty units that will perform better and last longer.

There are two general types of shock absorber in common use, with variations among brands and models. Most common is the type that utilizes oil as the shock-absorbing medium. The other, increasingly popular, is the type using a gas, almost always nitrogen. The latter may provide slightly more comfort and less control but it cannot (at this writing) be made adjustable for wear. Some oil shocks are adjustable for wear and ride hardness. Buy the replacement type recommended by the shock maker for your car unless you are radically changing either weight or weight distribution. You can spend six times as much as you did for the original equipment, but we believe it's worth the money.

Some rear shocks come with helper springs around them. These are for people who carry the vehicle's load limit on a regular basis. These helper springs save the spring from exceeding its capacity. There are air bag systems for this purpose, too.

About Springs | Springs themselves, whether coil, leaf, or torsion, sometimes get tired. Ordinarily, this is a problem that occurs well after the first 100,000 miles. Renewing the bushings and rubber isolators will be more rewarding, particularly since new, more effective components are being developed. A broken spring is rare, even in these days of potholes. If you believe that a pothole has damaged a spring (particularly the coil type), proceed to the nearest spring shop and let them find out for you. Ride quality deteriorates dramatically with a broken spring.

About Steering | We cannot overemphasize the need for constant checks, both on wheel alignment and for properly tight steering components. This will preserve ride and handling. There are ways to quicken steering by altering the pitman arm or other steering components. With power steering so prevalent, these become moot changes. Sometimes you can accomplish more by changing the power-steering fluid.

In fact, you can get a different "feel" if you change to a smaller or better steering wheel. With all due respect to the stock wheels, an elegant wood-and-steel or leather-wrapped steering wheel changes the equation. Get a matching gearshift knob if you have a floor-mounted shifting mechanism. If you don't and you'd like to have one, there are any number of kits for conversion from column to floor.

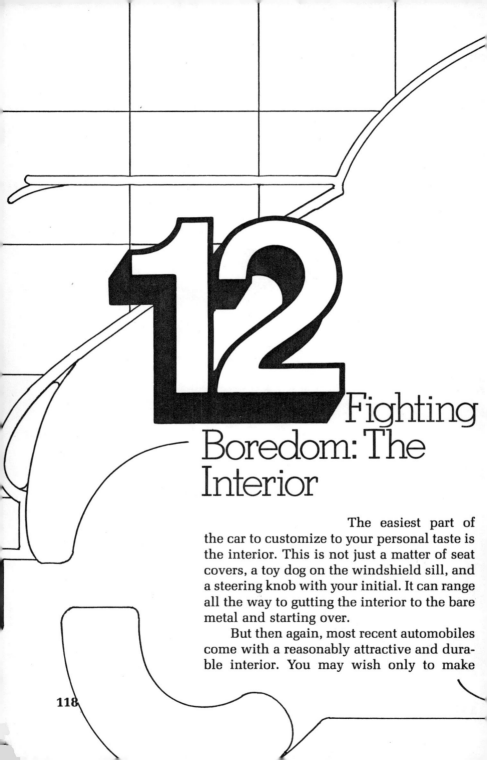

12 Fighting Boredom: The Interior

The easiest part of the car to customize to your personal taste is the interior. This is not just a matter of seat covers, a toy dog on the windshield sill, and a steering knob with your initial. It can range all the way to gutting the interior to the bare metal and starting over.

But then again, most recent automobiles come with a reasonably attractive and durable interior. You may wish only to make improvements that increase durability and reflect your tastes. That is why we have divided the possibilities into Mild Changes, Medium Changes, and Sky's the Limit. You can pick and choose according to your needs or desires. The idea is to make the interior so *simpático* that you not only will enjoy being in it but will actually look forward to being in it.

We will discuss sound systems in a separate chapter, because they become ever more important to the motorist slowing to save gas. There is more time spent getting from place to place, and car radios, or rather complete sound systems, help pass the time. Let's see what we can do with various components to upgrade the stock interior.

MILD CHANGES | For the person who wishes to add to or change the interior for relatively little money, we suggest that the first priority must be to add stuffing or otherwise improve the seats. Whether the vehicle is almost new or has been used for several years, the seats are likely to offer less than adequate support and durability. There are exceptions—some sports cars, a few sedans—but you will know immediately if your vehicle is one of these. For the great majority of vehicles, go to an auto upholsterer and ask him how much it would cost to add foam to the seats and the seat back and to reinforce the springs. If you find a real gem, he might even add reinforcement to the front-seat backs and improve thigh support by firming seat edges.

This is most necessary for front seats. In the majority of cars rear seating is used for less than 50 percent of all road miles. If this is true for you, forget about doing the rear.

If you are confident of your talent, you can stuff seats yourself. You need to remove the front seat and see if you can add material, stuffing from the bottom upwards. This may not be possible in some later model General Motors cars, which changed to a different kind of seating.

If you need to economize, stuff and repair the driver's side only. That's likely to have the most wear and sag—

and the occupant of that seat is most likely to be you.

Short of seat stuffing, purchase a ventilated back and seat support for each of the front sitting positions. Fasten each firmly into place by sewing in loops—but only after you have ascertained they improve support.

An alternative—if you are considering seat covers to hide wear and tears—is to pad under the seat cover but over the original seat facing. Reinforce the springs (if only with boards) and fasten the padding securely so it doesn't shift or bunch.

Good auto seating should support your thighs and your lower back. If you need to use pillows, that auto seating is not for you.

Another do-it-yourself project is repairing and re-painting a faded auto interior. There are special materials and paints made especially for fabric. Vinyl recoloring and repair kits can usually be found at your local notions store.

Upgrading the interior must make the automobile fit your size and weight so you can drive comfortably and safely. That can be difficult if you don't fall within the broad middle range of the population. When you start to customize, be aware that what will fit you may not fit other people using the car. Taller-than-normal people can get extended seat tracks, which let the seat slide further back. They also will find tilting seat backs a great aid. Either short or tall owners should investigate the availability of power seats when buying a new car, since the angle of both the seat and the back can create a better driving position for them.

Most people, incidentally, sit too close to the steering wheel when they drive. They look like a professional football linebacker crouched to pounce on a runner. Adjust the seat so that your arms are stretched almost full length, with elbows only slightly bent. The linebacker crouch is just a bad habit that needs to be broken for your own comfort. If you can't reach the pedals seated that far back, have blocks put on the pedals to make up the difference. Only the tiniest among us will need to do this.

A relatively minor change that also pays great dividends

has to do with the steering wheel. At the very least, cover the wheel with leather, PVC, or suede. You get a better grip and it looks classier. If you also wear driving gloves, you'll add to the feeling of increased control of the vehicle. Both minimize the "ice-cold or red-hot" syndrome caused by plastic steering wheels. Leave the driving gloves in the car so you won't lose them.

Another must is to improve vision for the driver. Keep the shelf under the rear window clear (totally—sudden stops turn objects on this shelf into deadly projectiles). Remove glare from your windshield shelf by one of a number of means—repaint it or add cloth (attached firmly). Keep extraneous items like the toy dog off there. Above all, clean off the film that clouds the inside of windshields and the rear-view mirror. If you smoke, you'll have to do it sooner, because the film forms quickly. If you have vinyl upholstery, you may do it sooner. If you sneeze or cough a great deal, you'll do it sooner.

Other methods of improving vision include adding a right side mirror—and adjusting it so you can see—adding an electric rear-window defroster if you live in a snowy clime, adding a tinted extension on your sun visor to forestall looking directly into the sun, and trying extenders for your rear-view mirror to eliminate the blind spots. If the car doesn't have it, buy a day-night rear-view mirror.

Another inexpensive way to upgrade the interior is to redo the dashboard—doing more than just cutting the glare. This can be with special paint (mask out instrument dials and warning lights first), with upholstery cloth or vinyl, or with adhesive-backed plastic. Cloth upholstery is expensive unless you do it yourself. Another way to change the dash is to add more instrumentation. Some suggestions are a tachometer, which tells you the engine's revolutions per minute (rpm), a windshield-wiper speed control, a real water-temperature gauge, and a real voltmeter. At this writing these can be had for well under $50 each, your installation.

Nonsmokers have one advantage: they can use the

ashtray as a coin receptacle. But they should so label it, even if only a few smokers drive or ride in the car. This brings us to a very useful way of upgrading vehicles with bucket seats—add a center console. If you buy it at your car dealer's, you may pay more, but you are more likely to get good fit and color match. Cars with bench seats and rear drives can be equipped with weighted saddles for the transmission hump; these have either an ashtray or a wastebasket, perhaps combined with a coin tray. A useful do-it-yourself project is to create and install center storage.

For mild changes, the most useful floor accessory is a set of floor mats. Get plastic or rubber if you track in mud or slush regularly. Remember, you'll need to shake the mats out regularly and clean them periodically. Get a good fit: if your car is a recent U.S. car, there is a set of mats that fits perfectly.

There is one further change you can effect in cars not already so equipped. Put carpet on the lower part of the doors, matching it to either the door color or the color of the floor carpeting. This is a boon to durability and looks, because it hides scuff marks made when getting in and out of the car.

MEDIUM | CHANGES

For those prepared to invest a little money to get the interior just right, we can suggest further candidates for change—for instance, steering wheels. The steering wheel in the car may be perfectly adequate, but it is a standard mass-produced size. You may feel more comfortable with a slightly smaller or larger wheel or a wheel with a thinner or thicker rim. Obviously, we are in a subjective area now: most people will have no physical reason to change the steering wheel, a change which can run $100 at this writing, with matching gear-shift knob. But always remember the reason behind these changes: to customize the interior and postpone the day when you feel you need to purchase a new car.

Steering wheels come in so many variations that you would be doing yourself a disservice not to consult the catalogues of more than one specialty house. The most popular wheels have either a woodfaced rim or a thick leather rim, both of which are easy to grip. If you are near an auto store that carries a custom line—some Sears outlets apparently do—go, look, and feel the wheels. Choose first for what feels good, second for what looks good—and then find out if it will fit your car. Wheels smaller in diameter are often more comfortable in cars equipped with power steering and afford greater clearance between you and the wheel. Steering wheels in a slightly larger diameter permit greater turning leverage for slow-speed maneuvers. Large wheels are most popular on vans and specialty vehicles, but some makes fit cars, too. If you want a larger steering wheel, make sure the inch of lost clearance does not cramp your seating position. If you have an adjustable steering column, this may not be a problem.

We mentioned seats before. You also can add sheepskin seat covers that, when tailored (not just the sheepskin held on with elastic straps), can easily run about $450, as we noted previously. We can attest to the fact that these are comfortable winter and summer. Get the darkest color possible, because light colors gather grime and need more care to keep new-looking.

As an alternative, you can reupholster, changing the entire seat facing. This is like reupholstering a living-room couch, but the padding and reconstruction are more critical. You really can let your imagination go free on fabric, vinyl, or leather, on pleating and quilting, and even on pillow style. Just remember that you must also have durability and ease of maintenance. Do the doors to match. It is hard to generalize about cost, but with a good auto upholsterer, we may be talking about $300 or more. You may find a regular upholsterer who is willing to do this work, but don't be his first such job unless you have the utmost confidence. Try to get more than one quote and more than one upholstery suggestion.

Recarpeting—or putting extra door-to-door carpeting above the present carpet—can serve a double purpose. The extra padding and thicker carpet will quiet the car. If you recarpet, insist on the thickest padding available and get a *minimum* of 18-ounce carpet. Anything less would be an exercise in futility. Unless you like maintenance, stay away from shag effects: they look great when new but don't stay that way long. Again, darker colors and neutral colors are preferable.

This is another chance to do it yourself if you are handy. Make a paper pattern of the area to be carpeted. Remove the front seat(s) to do this. Make it slightly oversize, so you can have carpet under the sills and back seat. If you are really handy, try bringing the carpet up the sides and front of the seats for a modern look. As we noted earlier, you can put carpeting on the doors, on the sidewalls, and under the dashboard, too. You will need to slit the carpet for seating rails, floor shift, and any through-the-floor pedals. Get a top-grade commercial carpeting and you'll get excellent wear.

One final suggestion is installation of a computer. These can be bought with from about 5 to over 50 functions; depending on the program, they will tell you how many miles before you run empty, based on your fuel consumption, miles traveled, miles to destination, miles per gallon, time traveled, average speed, and other information. They are the latest and best toy for the car, because they give useful information. The least expensive we have seen are under $100, the most, over $500. Check the number of functions and the ease of installation considering the number of functions. Most important of all, decide whether you are the type to program in the facts needed to start the computer working. It's not difficult, but some find it a bore to sit there and do it. Some computers will turn on the engine by remote command, open garage doors, and automatically turn off car lights. These are the more expensive units. Some imported vehicles may not be suitable for some of these computers because of emissions equipment or because they have a speedometer cable that rotates too fast (over 1045 rpm).

Of course you can add other useful instruments. We've suggested a tachometer already. If you have that, the next would be a vacuum gauge, which monitors vacuum at the carburetor. Both give you a way to adjust your driving style for greater efficiency and fuel economy. The tach will, for instance, tell you that you should get into the highest gear as quickly as possible (or, with an automatic transmission, if your transmission shift points are correct). The vacuum gauge will teach you to accelerate smoothly and to keep your range of speed as narrow as possible. There are types that actually have a dial divided into green (for economical driving) and red.

SKY'S THE LIMIT | We put total replacement of

front seats into this category, because for a Recaro seat with all the various adjustments automatic, you can pay $1,100 apiece. Another name brand, the Scheel, has a model at about $600, and it is easy to spend $400 per seat on any number of brand-name custom seats.

Such seats come in various widths—get the one that fits your shape—and constructions. Most have lumbar supports that can be adjusted; some have adjustments on thigh support and even shoulder support. All those that we have examined seemed to have good head protection. With a custom seat, you are looking not only for comfort but also for lateral support that holds you steady no matter how twisty or bumpy the road, no matter how quickly you need to accelerate. In combination with your shoulder harness, you should expect their superior construction would also afford more safety.

The only way to decide if such seating is for you is to sit in it and drive. Although it is illogical, many of these seats are sold without such a test. As with any major purchase, check several brands and several models before you buy. Stores and dealers that specialize in such seats may also have seats they took out of new cars that you can buy and use. Check this possibility, too. It may be a better deal for your taste.

Replacing the headliner, particularly with a one-piece foam-covered plastic piece, is a way to quiet and modernize your car. Car dimensions didn't change for years, so you may be able to do this easily with a stock liner. A more expensive alternative is padding the interior ceiling. Combined with well-padded floors and doors, this will create the quiet that people associate with luxury. Another candidate for sound-proofing is the firewall separating the passenger and engine compartments. *Lead* foil is perhaps the optimum in sound-proofing without adding undue weight. Undercoating is also effective.

Don't forget the trunk in redoing your vehicle's interior. You can carpet it, upholster it, build in compartments, or add an auxiliary fuel tank (if of approved construction). In station wagons, the sidewalls often offer added chance for storage.

Sun roofs and moon roofs cost up to $750 at this writing. They vary tremendously, so we'll only mention some of the generalized salient points.

- You lose headroom with all except the most inexpensive installations.

- Moon roofs, which are translucent or tinted see-through panels, may let in more light and make the car interior feel larger, but only the best installations retain roof strength.

- Sun roofs, which are opaque, come hand-operated or electric, at all price levels and with many varying features. Get something decent or you run the risk of water leaks and intrusion of heat or cold.

- Try to see an installation before buying. Don't buy any sun roof that doesn't solve the problem of "thrum-ming," a buffeting noise caused by air rushing into the opening at speed. The usual solution is a windbreak, either a pop-up type or one you can attach when the panel is removed or wound back.

You also can get a kit that converts hand-cranked windows to electric. These must be installed neatly and correctly. We do not advocate electric windows, especially considering the cost of after-market installations. They complicate the inner door and if they break you can't roll the window down.

A total redoing of the interior from the bare metal out usually is reserved for special-purpose cars, but if you really like the performance and dimensions of what you have, consider it. You will have to have a minimum of about $1,500 (at this writing) to invest. The sky's the limit if someone else does it, but anyone who has upholstered a living-room set himself can attempt this successfully. Plan everything beforehand, from what you will use for underlayment to how you are going to do the door panels to where you will put the hidden storage.

These are just some of the major possibilities for upgrading the interior. A look at a mail-order auto-house catalog will suggest others. Think about them carefully before you buy.

13

Fighting Boredom: Auto Sound

The automobile radio is only some five decades old. Today's ambulatory concert halls and rolling sound studios are only one decade old. Currently, we demand a level of performance and sophistication from auto sound systems that was unheard of in home units a relatively short time ago.

And we should. We believe that anyone who is not tone-deaf should have a radio that reproduces sound with high fidelity. Whether or not you wish stereophonic FM as well as AM depends upon where you live. It may be pointless to get AM-FM stereo with Dolby effect if the nearest FM station is 200 miles away. But it is never pointless to have a built-in eight-track stereo cartridge unit or a cassette unit. You can be in the most remote parts of this country and bring your music or dramatic readings with you.

It is also never pointless to be equipped with a citizen's band (CB) radio, not to help you avoid speed traps but to use as a safety device. CB can report your position in case you have some kind of emergency—medical, car problems, or any other. It can permit you to be a good citizen safely, reporting road blockages, traffic jams, accidents, or break-downs along the road.

Finally, a complete sound system can help get you through traffic jams or those long lonely trips calmer and more relaxed, which will help you to drive at legal speeds as a matter of course. We believe it's the number-one weapon in fighting boredom with your current set of wheels. When you have the sound system just right in a particular car, you will be very reluctant to give it up.

You can build a car system the same way as you would one for your home—with separate tape deck, tuner, amplifi-er, frequency equalizers, and so forth. Unless you have a home system of similar sophistication, however, we urge you to simply concentrate on an AM-FM tape unit. The radio will incorporate the amplifier, tuner, and a number of other components.

This one decision makes an impossible task possible. Now you need to decide how much you want to spend and what fits your car. You will most likely revise the former upward; the only way to decide the latter is to listen to various systems. What you seek is distortion-free sound, without the cyclic variations that make sound tinny, thin, or wobbly. No matter how many car-stereo salesmen you meet, remember the basic priority: it must be within your capacity to pay and it must sound good to you—not only with the store's demo tape but with your tape (bring it along clearly marked as yours), and not only on some FM station that the store selects but on the one you listen to.

Also remember that the system has to fit into your car. If you don't have room for that $1,100 system the salesman showed you, chances are you can do almost as well with something more compact and much less expensive. Remember that the sound in a car is in a more restricted space than in your home. You do not need 60 watts of power per channel in your Chevette, GLC, or Phoenix; 10 to 20 watts will do.

Let's go over the main and subsidiary ingredients of a sound system briefly, trying to improve it with the least hassle and cost. These are:

1) Radio and aerial

2) Speakers

3) Tape unit

4) Booster and other special-effects devices

5) CB unit and aerial

Radio and Aerial | This is the basic sound unit. If your car has an AM-FM or AM-FM-tape unit already in it, you can bring out its full potential by relocating your present speakers or adding or substituting better ones. But if you don't have a unit or if you want to invest in a more advanced or more compact sound unit, you are in the marketplace.

As we said, your tastes and your geographic location should dictate your choice of replacement radio. The newer electronic units are smaller yet have more capabilities, and the chances are they will continue to be miniaturized so they will fit whatever car you own. Before you buy, however, think about features. For instance, do you need signal seeking, which searches automatically for stations with strong radio signals and their exact position on the radio band, if you hardly stray from a metro area where there are many stations? You do need to be locked exactly on the station (96.3 instead of 96.0, as an example) if you listen to FM regularly. Do you need a local/distance switch? Do you need multiplex sound if there are no stations broadcasting in multiplex? How many stations do you listen to regularly? Are four programmable pushbuttons enough, or do you need five? Or none?

Most radios have some kind of balance control. They are usually to accommodate left and right speakers. Another control, called either tone or balance, is for treble to bass. If you have speakers in the doors you are in good shape regarding tonal balance. If you have speakers both in the doors and the rear (four-speaker systems), you also need a fader switch for front-to-rear balance. If you have one speaker in the dashboard only, you don't need a radio with left-right balance control.

Should you buy a radio with tape built in? There are two common systems: eight-track and cassette. You must choose one or the other. Do you listen regularly to tapes? Would you like to? Buy the built-in. In fact, if you can fit such a unit in (and can find it), buy a combination that has AM, FM multiplex, CB, and tape.

How do you know which radio to buy, after you have decided on the features you wish? Check the following points of comparison—audio power (wattage), sensitivity (it's different for AM and FM·in a given unit), and frequency response.

Audio power is the capacity to reproduce all the tones from bass to treble.

Frequency response is how far into the bass and treble the radio can reproduce clearly.

Sensitivity is the signal to reduce the tuner's noise and distortion to a specified decibel level. The lower the figure, the better, because then you can hear faraway FM stations better.

We are not going to give a course in high fidelity; if you are serious about sound you should read up on it or ask questions. Instead, we are going to present a baseline of a reasonable AM-FM stereo unit at this writing.

Audio power: 9 watts at 10 percent THD (distortion level) or 7.5 watts at 1 percent THD

Frequency response: 75 to 10,000 Hertz

AM sensitivity for 20 decibels: 20 microvolts

FM sensitivity for 30 decibels: 15 microvolts

Buy your setup in a place where you can hear the sound. Your car dealer's is one place; auto sound dealers now put up displays at auto shows and custom-car shows. Above all, talk to some experts about your needs and desires.

The aerial is often neglected. If you don't have a high-quality aerial—maybe with a booster—you are not going to pick up as strong a signal. This is just as important in the city, where tall buildings may give trouble, as in the wide-open spaces. It is especially important with FM. However, it is likely that your present aerial is suitable if your present sound is AM-FM. Otherwise, check the experts. (You can convert the radio to use an aerial other than the one in the windshield, or you can buy a booster mechanism to improve that kind of aerial.) For the serious listener, even the best aerial will not eliminate FM multipath distortion and ghosts all the time. Go to tape players.

Speakers | The easiest way to tell which kind of speakers you are getting is by the weight of the woofer magnet and the speaker's ability to match the audio power of your radio. If you have a radio or tape system that can deliver 25 watts per channel, you need speakers that can translate that amount of wattage into sound. If you have a system with occasional peaks at 50 watts—that can be loud enough to wake your ancestors—you need such speakers. If the speakers can't, poof—they will blow out. A larger magnet usually means more capacity.

If you want stereo sound, you will need at least two

speakers, one for each side. Each speaker must be able to reproduce at least the range of your radio.

Let's start at the low end and work up. The least expensive are dual-cone speakers. These are single woofer units that have a small megaphone near their center. This is supposed to enhance the clarity of treble sounds and distribute them. A two-way speaker has a woofer for the bass and a tweeter for the high notes built into the same unit. They share the same magnet. A coaxial system combines separate woofer and tweeter with a crossover. Each will have its own magnet. Even more expensive are three-way units, with a midrange component added. The most complex and expensive at this writing divide the sound into five ranges and provide a separate component for each. We have listened to this and, to us at least, it does not justify the added cost. Road noise and motor noise mask refinements beyond a certain point, so you need to be parked and running on battery to get full use.

How many speakers do you need? For small cars, left and right full-range speakers of good quality are more than adequate if properly located. Add a pair of tweeters up front, and you have about as good a combination as most car owners can appreciate. Tweeter modules are easily obtained and will mount in doors, the dash, or the ceiling.

Where the speakers are located is of critical importance, so get them installed by experts or at least get advice before chopping and cutting interior panels.

Why is the shelf under the rear window a favorite location for speakers? Because there's plenty of space there and the trunk acts as a sound chamber. What if you own a sports car or station wagon or hatchback? Mount the speakers in doors, in the sidewall, or in the ceiling—or get hang-on units to install where heads and cargo won't hit them.

Tape Unit I As we said, the first choice for anyone must be the all-in-one installation. Whether it's all-in-one or separate, however, you have a choice of eight-track or cassette tape deck. The cassette now is more popular because it is more compact, it rewinds to either end of the tape and is generally much higher fidelity because of the nature of the cassette-playing mechanism. Some cassette decks have automatic rewind and eject features. Some will automatically play the other side of the tape, saving you the need to flip the cassette. Up until recently eight-track offered a wider selection of musical and talking tapes, but this is no longer true.

If you are adding a separate under-dash component, we would still recommend a cassette. Anchor it far more securely than the mounting provided with the unit—and locate it so you can reach it easily from the driver's seat.

Whether you choose all-in-one or a separate component, try to compare signal-to-noise ratio. Many deck specs don't quote this figure, because it gives a relative amount of background noise for any loudness setting and makes comparison simple. A high db (decibel) number means the signal is strong against background noise. About 35 to 40 is acceptable, but the higher the better. Ask a stereo salesperson about the signal-to-noise ratio of a given tape unit, and if he or she doesn't know what you're talking about, get a different person to help: either the one you asked is no expert or he's concealing something.

Some salesmen will quote wow and flutter figures. Wow and flutter are words that sound exactly like the problems they represent. Unless you're in the $1,000-plus range, ignore these because WRM (the weighted figure) and RM (the unweighted figure for wow and flutter) are so low on any good cassette deck that the average ear won't notice a variation.

Booster and Other Special-Effects Devices | Here are some

of the add-ons that can enhance your system once you hunger for even more enjoyable sound. A booster amplifier adds wattage to the system; if your system has noise or distortion it will amplify that, too. In most cases, however, it helps. If you're buying a booster, you may as well buy it combined with a frequency equalizer. This is a lovely adult toy that, instead of merely permitting you to select treble or bass, widens the selection to fine-tuning five frequency ranges or more. If you get the kind with a visual display, you'll see a wave pattern, too, as well as hear it. All of these come with fader controls, permitting front-to-rear as well as left-to-right adjustment. Do not boost the wattage beyond speaker capacity. You will merely blow up your speakers.

For that Carnegie Hall or Hollywood Bowl sound, you can add a reverb or delay unit. This must be adjusted properly, because what it does is electronically delay some sound frequencies a microsecond to create the effect of sound reverberating in a concert hall.

CB Unit and Aerial

Although some AM-FM-CB units have surfaced for installation in new cars, the chances are 99 to 1 you won't pay out this kind of money to add CB. Separate CB installations are much more likely. While CB as a fad has faded, CB as a road and emergency communications system continues to grow more necessary. More and more police departments monitor various channels and announce this fact in signs. It extends their ability to respond to breakdowns and get help to you. As noted before, it extends your ability to report dangerous road conditions or warn people away from traffic jams.

The range of CB varies from ½ mile in congested urban areas to 5 miles or more on open rural road. That fact has nothing to do with your equipment's quality. What does have to do with it is the antenna you have, its location, and the ability of the unit to receive and send with minimum noise and maximum clarity.

Never skimp on your antenna. CB is legally limited to a maximum of four watts of transmitting power, so you need all the help you can get from the antenna. The most practical is a four-foot metal or fiberglass-base loaded type with a spring mount that can be attached to the trunk lid or to a hatchback roof. Usually the wand is removable, and sometimes the whole antenna is a clip-on unit. The risk of theft is large enough so that you must be able to leave it inside the locked car. The long (9-foot) whip antennas that mount on bumpers may give slightly wider range, but they are prone to break. At this writing, the newest antennas had coil boosters to send and gather the signals from further away.

The sending and receiving unit, which contains the channel selection blanker, S meter, and squelch control, is called a transceiver. Buy it last. Most are excellent in performance, but you'll pay for the brand name. The transceiver will come with a microphone. Trade it in or give it away and get a pre-amp mike or power mike, which amplifies your signal, thus gaining distance and loudness. Have an expert make the switch for you; soldering is involved.

Some mikes have the channel selector incorporated, thus letting you switch with a flick of your thumb. This is convenient, considering that you may also wish to drive the car or van.

The final items in your mobile CB setup may be the so-called extras, most of which do you no good if you buy the full 43-channel transceiver. Make the salesman justify the extra money for the likes of boosters and permanent SWR meters.

Once you get a CB, remember that even if a license is no longer required, the FCC is monitoring. Learn what you can and cannot do with citizen's band. If they or their mobile strike force nail you, ignorance of the law is no excuse. Ten-four.

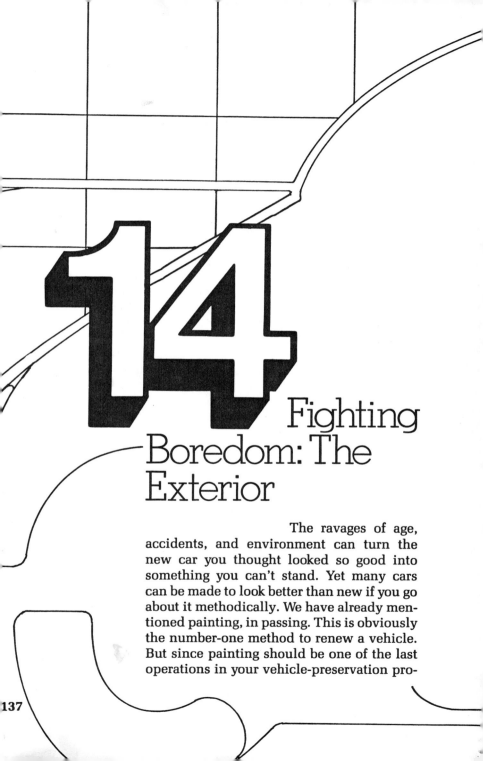

14

Fighting Boredom: The Exterior

The ravages of age, accidents, and environment can turn the new car you thought looked so good into something you can't stand. Yet many cars can be made to look better than new if you go about it methodically. We have already mentioned painting, in passing. This is obviously the number-one method to renew a vehicle. But since painting should be one of the last operations in your vehicle-preservation program, that's when we'll discuss it. Any changes in the sheet metal and accessories should be made first.

The very first thing you should do is look at your car as though you were a used-car buyer trying to knock down the price. Find all the nicks and dents, the places where the bubbles of rust have appeared, the dull spots. Try to remember if this was the color you really wanted when you bought the car or whether there is a preferable color. What about the trim? Do you like the "chrome," or would a different rub strip or brightwork effect look better? Why not leave off the rub strip? Does the body have metal accent lines stamped in? Would it look better if they were deemphasized or filled? Was there a later model with basically the same sheet metal that you thought was particularly handsome? Do you prefer the look of a more deluxe model of your car or a sister car? Have you thought about two-toning, striping, or both?

We have mentioned a wide number of stratagems. Some need expert aid, while others may be helped along by a visit to your friendly junkyard. Let's examine these. Again, we'll go from least expensive to more expensive, more radical updating. And the least has to be removing the rub strips.

Before you do anything, plan what you want to accomplish. As you investigate the possibilities, make notes; when things get advanced enough, try to sketch your plan or get a picture of your car and draw on it. The idea is to forestall extra work.

Many U.S. cars, particularly notch-roof sedans (those with a visible trunk), look better with a side panel unbroken by the rub strip. If there are no accent creases in the side metal, these vehicles may look more elegant, especially if the roofline is squarish. Sedans with rooflines showing virtually no break between roof and tail to differentiate the trunk are called fastbacks and they don't usually gain in looks by removing the rub strip. But station wagons may. The notch roof is "in," however, and likely will stay "in" because it affords most headroom. Removing rub strips from hatchbacks—a hatchback's entire rear lifts like a clam opening up—may improve the appearance.

Most U.S. cars built in 1977 or later have the rub strips bonded on, so there should be no attachment hole; but if you see a screw at one end of the rub strip, forget this stratagem unless you are willing to repaint or touch up. Similarly, if you find that the rub strip is attached by hidden clips, push it back on unless you are willing to repaint or at least stripe the vehicle. Bonded-on rub strips may be removed more or less easily by peeling them off once you have worked a tip loose. If you are adamant and remove rub strips held by clips or screws, fill the holes with any of a number of plastic fillers, sand down the filler, and either touch up the repair or cover it with striping.

The next least expensive option is to relocate the rub strip or to change its width, depth, and color. This can be an intriguing exercise as you search for a rub strip or striping location that pleases you. The most methodical way to do this is to make a paper pattern of the side of your car from front to rear. You can buy plain wrapping paper and roll it out, taping it to the entire side of the car. You can also save shopping bags, cut them open, and tape them together; they are heavier paper. Now you can proceed two ways. You can draw on the paper in pencil (use a yardstick and try to make it straight). Or you can hold or tape the removed rub strip in the position that you feel might look better.

Moving it closer to metal creases, which are accent lines that strongly affect the car's look, will deemphasize the molding; moving it up toward the beltline will make the car look bulkier. The beltline is an imaginary place just below the topline of the fender and doors. On a monotone car, moving the rub strip down toward the wheel well emphasizes the greenhouse (windows, pillars, and roof) and, depending on the location of metal creases, generally makes the vehicle look higher and/or shorter. You can fight these tendencies by varying the color and using pinstriping. Two-tone the car at the crease of the upper fender (the hood and rear deck should be the same color as the roof and pillars) and put contrasting pinstripes at the place where the colors join. Having a light greenhouse and a darker body makes the vehicle look lower and longer and bulkier. A darker greenhouse will make it appear taller. With this treatment, if you move the molding higher, you can then counteract the tendency to height. You will see the difference at once.

If you would rather not spend your time cutting up shopping bags, you have the option of strolling through a shopping center, parking lot, or auto show. Look at the various cars most like yours in shape. Pick the brains of the car-company stylists by analyzing how they manage different appearances. Or if you see a style, color, or different molding treatment you especially like, write down its particulars and duplicate it.

There are a number of other stratagems for particular purposes. For instance, putting a bright molding on the rocker panel and around the wheel wells will lengthen a boxy car. Blacking out the rocker panels (you can do that with undercoating spray if you mask the paint nearby) and outlining the wheel wells in black also makes the vehicle look longer and racier. For the macho look, get the window moldings, side mirrors, and windshield wipers painted matte black, too. But let the bumpers stay bright, along with the wheels or wheelcovers.

Another way to make a vehicle look longer is by painting a contrast stripe 3 inches wide or wider across the entire side of the car. On hatchbacks, 4½ or 5 inches is fine. Most wagons, however, look strange if you do this. If you want to emphasize the length of a wagon, try the more conventional simulated wood grain vinyl paneling rather than wide striping.

Pinstriping is another relatively inexpensive way to change a vehicle. However, whether you choose a vinyl stripe or one that is painted on, it should be applied after you have completed painting or other alterations. Larger cars usually look better with dual stripes along or near the beltline down the entire length of the side. These should taper to a single point in front, and most importantly should not clash with but complement any metal accent lines or chrome you are retaining.

A unifying effect is achieved with a pinstripe that continues around the rear of the car or even around its entire periphery. This treatment combines well with two-toning but also works on its own. Exact placement of such pinstriping is quite important. If you are having it done professionally, ask the stripe person where he's going to place the stripe—99½ times out of 100 he'll be right. One exception is the late-1970s Chevy Monte Carlo; the pinstripe there should follow the downward curve of the front fender, then break, and then follow the metal crease in the rear quarter panel. Another example of an exception is the mid-1970s Cadillac, where pinstriping should be just above the rub strip.

The other common use of pinstriping is for outlining the shape of the body side or hood or greenhouse. This treatment, which is used mostly to make trucks and vans look less formidable, is possible and popular for late-1970s Mercuries and Lincolns or any car with knife-edge styling (a sharp break between the vertical and horizontal surfaces). A good pinstriper can transform a Rabbit or Scirocco with this kind of treatment.

The effects gained by deemphasizing or filling accent lines stamped into metal all depend on your sense of judgment regarding a particular model. For instance, Ford intermediate-size vehicles of the mid-1970s have metal accent lines. They could be deemphasized by feathering (with filler), but the end result is such a subtle change that the effort hardly seems worthwhile. However, Mustangs of that era have a side-panel indent. Deemphasizing it by feathering into the indent or by filling the indent with Styrofoam and then smoothing the surface with filler gives you a whole new look. It is perhaps better to try less-ambitious projects first.

Filler can be utilized to enhance appearance wherever panels join, assuming there is nothing going up and down or in and out. Most late-model vehicles, U.S. and import, have two types of joints that cry for filling and smoothing. The first category includes joints between the front panel and the hood and fenders, and between either the rear panel or the fender extenders and the rear fenders or quarter panels. These separations act as a visual stop sign to the impression the eye has of length. Where they are not working joints—as with some hoods—filling them in before repainting adds smoothness and visual length to any car. Often it's a case of joining plastic and metal, but there are fillers that can do this.

The other kind of joint that begs for better finishing is the place where panels come together at the cowl or rear deck and the fenders. These are filled at the factory but not fully. With an older car this filler may have shrunk. Clean it all out and refill. The best filler is lead filler, but some body shops claim it is difficult to obtain. There are Bondex or plastic filler, caulking compounds, fiberglass-reinforced fillers, and a graphite-reinforced caulk in the works that is said to strengthen the vehicle as you improve its cosmetics. If you do nothing else except make these joints disappear, you will have changed the lines of your car for the better.

MOVING BETTER THROUGH AIR

We now touch on the science of aerodynamics, which for our purposes can be defined as getting the vehicle through the air in the most efficient manner. Why is this a benefit? Because then you use less fuel to attain any speed. Researchers at the car companies have found this important, and not just at high speeds. Aerodynamic flaws—perhaps a windshield at the wrong angle —can cost 1 mpg or more. Examine the newest cars: many of the changes they have made you can't do unless you wish to buy a whole new body skin—and, until the new cars reach the junkyards in greater numbers, this is prohibitively expensive to do panel by panel. But you can pick up ideas that are possible. For instance, window moldings: on new cars these tend to be thinner, flatter, and merge smoothly into sheet metal. By some estimates here is a potential gain of 1 mpg. If fuel is $1.50 per gallon and you get 20 mpg and you drive 10,000 miles a year, just such a small improvement contributes $37.50 toward the cost of the change in the first year.

You may have thought that wheel openings are becoming smaller. They may look it, but we're told they really aren't. The edges are contoured differently and the tire is closer to the edge of the opening because the airflow along the side of the car should not be interrupted there. Front valance panels—the part under your front bumper—control airflow under the car, and in some cases rocker panels have been shaped to deflect water and air. Rub strips are flatter, too.

If you wish to improve fuel economy while altering appearance subtly, try having a front air dam or valance panel fashioned of elastomeric (rubbery) material for your car. You want a front skirt under the bumper and extending around to the side about as far as the bumper. Since it should be lower than your current valance panel, just low enough so that it will occasionally contact driveways (a normal clearance of 3 or 4 inches), cut it out of PVC, neoprene, or plain old heavy rubber carpet roll. You can make a pattern out of paper, fit it to the car, and figure attachment places; or the person who works on your car can. Some imports and a few domestics have air dams built for them, which are sold either at the dealer or at a specialty shop. Check that possibility if you're not building it yourself. Air dams improve air flow by letting less air under the car, but we're not promising miracles; you are not going to turn a 10-mpg guzzler into a fuel-economy champion this way. You will see deeper air dams more and more on new cars, however, since the car makers realize this is beneficial, too.

LOOK AT THE RELATIVES

One of the better methods of forming judgments on color, on striping, and on updating generally is to look at sister cars and other models of the same car as your own. For most domestics and some imports, this gives you a wide choice of what professional designers feel is attractive. For instance, if you have a Chevrolet Caprice, its sister cars are the Pontiac Bonneville, the Olds Delta 88, and the Buick LeSabre. You need not pick up an entire style: that may entail buying or finding too many parts. But you can pick up color treatments and variety in styles of moldings. Since the basic body changes little for as long as seven years, you can imagine tremendous variety in these elements. Similarly, you can update or upgrade from lower to higher price within the given model. For instance, 1977, 1978, and 1979 Caprices had the same sheet metal, but the grille and tail lenses changed. If you have an Impala (the lower-priced car in the model line), you may be able to give it Caprice touches. Other possible examples of sister cars among those made in the United States are Chrysler, Plymouth, and Dodge (depending on model and year); Mercury and Ford across the entire line below Lincoln; Skylark and Omega front-wheel drives; Citation and Phoenix front-wheel drives; Lincoln and the Continental Mark series (some components); Monza and Sunbird.

Should you enjoy an abundance of either money or ideas, it is possible to reskin by fashioning body parts out of reinforced plastic. But the government will be watching to make sure it's not meant for production. Production bodies are subject to safety regulations, and to the same testing that the Detroit manufacturer gets.

Another popular way to transform a car is with a vinyl roof. That no longer means merely covering the roof and pillars with vinyl. There are many variations:

- The conventional vinyl roof.

- The padded full vinyl roof. This permits changing roof contours to something more formal. On some cars it permits a frameless rear window.

- The padded full roof with altered quarter-panel treatment. Again, elegance is sought; the car with the split rear side window setup usually gets an opera window treatment reminiscent of Gay Nineties carriages, imposed behind the split of the rear window.

- The half roof with or without Targa strip. This looks

excellent on some coupes like Grand Prix and Monte Carlo. A Targa strip is a wide bright metal band forward of the leatherette.

- The padded cabriolet roof either full formal with no opera window, or with an opera window.

- The fake convertible roof. Some cars look very good with a canvas top, which masks rust around the windows.

Vinyl or "canvas" roofs do not add much soundproofing. Nor are they particularly durable. Nor do they diminish car maintenance, since you must use protectant and special cleaner. But they do give you a wide range of options for decor. All vinyls or canvases are not alike. Various grains or weaves are available, from wild alligator to a very formal whipcord effect. Roof fabrics should either pick up some interior color or match the color of the car. The rub strip, either wide and padded or narrow, should match the roof vinyl. If you attempt the padded stylized continental-wheel rear-end treatment—as on some Mercury Cougars and Lincoln Versailles—that also should match.

The way to proceed is to find a shop that does roofs, pick the expert's brain on prices, color matches, and grains. Ask him if he can do padded roofs with built-up edges. A good roof shop often includes an auto upholsterer who can match interior components with the roof. It is much more difficult to match the roof with the interior, since the grain in the vinyl in the doors and on the dash may well be obsolete. If you try this, confine your alligator grains to door panels; finer-grained patterns may be used more extensively.

Plan It All Out | Even if you feel this updating of your car will be a task lasting several years, plan the entire job out so you know almost specifically what end result you wish. It is why we have saved painting for last. Few will attempt other more radical solutions—for instance, rebodying vehicles totally with car kits—because most kits are for a chassis like the VW. And still fewer will attempt to design and mold fiberglass replacement parts, because these require expertise in proper reinforcement and finishing.

Finally, only certain cars can sustain the massive chromed grilles and other accouterments that make for exhibitionism. Thus, painting is usually part of the plan that you complete before trying much beyond playing with the rub strip. Plan what you want carefully; we reiterate: sketch it. Draw it in detail if you have that talent or know someone who has. Then realize that for a car that must last and last, there is no such animal as an economy paint job *unless* either you are fickle or you are retaining the same or a similar color.

We strongly recommend a superior job. What's that? The paint shop will remove as much of the chrome as possible, carefully masking windows and any brightwork that is difficult to remove. They paint door sills and door edges, pillars, fender inners, and even the inside of hood and trunk lids—which is quite important if you are changing color. They also paint wheels to match. Usually, they have a wide selection of colors, are not afraid of two-toning and can match the present color, if you wish to retain it. Also, they will machine-sand either the entire car or the area to be painted and do some specific hand sanding as well. They will fill where it's needed, and the resulting job will be free of drips, ripples, runs, or dried-in dust. This kind of job may cost five or six times as much as the economy paint job, but it will look as good as the original and, given good maintenance, it will last and last. If you see chrome painted over, you are looking at what was probably an economy job. Tell the painter beforehand that you want sills, hood, and fender inners painted. That way there won't be any misunderstanding over the job or the price.

One step still more expensive is the custom painter, who will create special effects or give your Mercedes 450 SL a 16-coat paint job that looks so magnificent and deep that you'll resent every speck of dust and hate every bird above. You can get part of that deep effect with clear coating, which utilizes no pigment over the final color coat. Smaller cars can accept special-effects paint jobs better. When you seek such special effects, get a color drawing or—if you can find one—a picture of an actual car. Special effects range from multi-color V-stripes to black that fades to yellow from the rear forward.

You can add bulldog or lady or rocket hood ornaments as a further decoration, but they seem to be out of style, as are fake hood scoops. Functional hood scoops—if you are attempting a ram air system—should be located for maximum ram effect: get an expert. A ram air system uses the forward motion of the vehicle to force extra air into the carburetor for improved high-speed performance. It also has the secondary effect of dissipating engine heat faster. The only disadvantage we can think of is that water may come in if it's raining hard enough. Should the system be improperly specified and installed, it isn't going to hurt anything. It just won't work.

And then there are roof racks. Any car will sustain some kind of roof rack, but unless you actually use the rack regularly you are going to ruin your aerodynamics and use more fuel. Some permanent racks are designed to minimize this flaw, but the removable kind will do the job on occasional trips. The same goes for racks for skis, bikes, and boats.

We have not touched upon side mirrors either. These also offer a chance to make the vehicle more aerodynamic and modern-looking. There is such a wide variety of styles that all we can say is investigate what fits your car both physically and visually. Nor have we said much about fender skirts—which, we are told, may make a comeback for aerodynamic reasons.

The way your car finally looks and how you think other people react will determine how successfully you fight the programmed urge to trade in or sell long before usefulness is done. If you plan ahead and plan well, this urge will never arise until you really and truly see a product of a much higher order of sophistication, beauty, and efficiency. Remember, planning before doing gives you a better chance at satisfaction. Remember also to consider all the stratagems within your means. Settling for anything less is like buying a chocolate cream pie, putting a slice on your plate, and then just sitting and staring at it.

15

Thinking about the Future

Let's face reality. Somewhere down the road the advances in automotive technology and other factors may seem to indicate that the purchase of a new automobile is the best answer to your transport needs. Judging by what we know is on the drawing boards for the near future, we believe you can take steps short of vehicle purchase, but that is our personal judgment. Some new automobile may be attractive and

efficient enough to make you decide to buy it. Or your
transport needs may change radically and the vehicle you
have worked to preserve may no longer be suitable.

These are powerful arguments for change unless they
are counterbalanced by the greater passenger or cargo space
you may now have, unless you again figure in financing costs
for a new car (see Appendix Three), or unless you have not
found a way to control current maintenance costs. The most
powerful factor of all, we reiterate, is the need to replace any
vehicle that has been in a major accident.

In these times, you are at the mercy of forces you as an
individual cannot control. We have known for years that cars
can be powered by alcohols, either methanol from coal,
wood, or garbage and animal wastes, or ethanol from
sugarcane, grains (corn especially), whey, and crop chaff.
The reason given previously for not developing alcohols for
fuels commercially was that it was not as cheap as gas or oil.
That is no longer true and, despite obstacles, we are fast
increasing our supply of gasohol (90 percent unleaded gas,
10 percent ethanol). According to the "experts," that 9:1
ratio is about all that most current engines will burn without
modifications. According to other "experts," the amount of
ethanol needed for widespread use of gasohol is about all
America can produce without reducing the food supply.
According to the number-one ethanol producer, Archer-
Daniels-Midland, ethanol may be obtained with no reduc-
tion in the food supply.

We have some questions about the motives of such
"experts." How can any "expert" declare that ethanol
production must be limited to corn and sugarcane now in
the food chain? Other parts of the biomass can be utilized. A
decade ago, Nebraska University scientists were using wheat
chaff and corn stalks and leavings to make ethanol. Right
now we let more grain and other foods spoil than we would
need to make the alcohol for gasohol. We need an organized
effort to retrieve that spoiled food. The real truth is we can
make as much ethanol as we want to make. DNA research
could make petroleum obsolete as a fuel.

And who says the engine of your car can't be modified? It has been modified to meet so-called pollution and gas-mileage rules the hard way—by adding expensive components. The car companies already know how to modify your engine to run on 20 percent ethanol, 50 percent ethanol —whatever.

If, moreover, Americans become logical and force a switch to alcohols as the basic automotive fuel instead of gasoline, it is well within the capability of any major car company to build engines particularly suited to the advantages and shortcomings of these inexhaustibly renewable fuels, whether methanol or ethanol.

We are talking about modified versions of the engine in your car. But every major U.S. company can also build you a turbine engine that will burn your favorite perfume if necessary to keep you mobile. These multi-fuel engines are a whisker away from being more fuel-efficient than a diesel, and they emit far fewer pollutants. You won't get one in a car anytime soon. It might imperil the people in government and in industry who become obsolete the minute such an engine is introduced commercially. Yes, burning alcohol in this or any engine will produce less of what we call power for the amount burned. But since the fuel burns more completely—in other words, you get more of the power there is in the alcohol—you may not notice the difference. In even your present engine, the 10 or 50 percent alcohol fuel burns more completely, so there may be no need for some power-robbing emission gear. You might like that—but consider the sad plight of the vast numbers employed by the emissions-hardware industry.

So while countries with a much smaller technological base like Brazil may well accomplish a switch to alcohol, there is little sign that Americans are ready to demand this of their government. Nor is the energy-distribution system anxious to change the status quo. Gasohol is just the tip of the iceberg, and already the organized energy-distribution system has been trying in every way possible to sabotage its acceptance. For every Texaco and Sunoco "experiment" or trial sale, there are myriad roadblocks including lawsuits and harassment of franchisees who wish to sell gasohol. Not only that, but as of this writing the oil lobby has conducted a vicious propaganda campaign attacking alcohol-based fuels. Can you imagine how they would react should some brave corporate soul propose to take us totally off the oil addiction and OPEC dependency?

Therefore, unless you wish to get a license from the government to operate a still to make ethanol "for scientific transportation purposes" (you can), you must worry about the impact of fuel costs on your vehicle. If fuel reaches $2.50 a gallon, even the best-maintained 12-to-14-mpg vehicle has a major cost penalty attached to it. We include in Appendix Two a table on annual fuel costs at various prices per gallon for 5,000, 7,500, and 10,000 miles. Say you have checked and you believe you are averaging 20 mpg. Your cost for fuel alone at $1.25 is approximately $312 for every 5,000 miles you drive—or $625 for 10,000 miles and $937 for 15,000 miles. For $2.50-per-gallon fuel, double those costs —$625, $1,250, and $1,994. That's for a 20-mpg car. The figures for a 14-mpg gallon vehicle at $2.50 per gallon, as you will see, are $893, $1,786, and $2,679. The figures at $2.50 a gallon for a 27.5-mpg vehicle (the 1985 federal corporate average fuel economy goal) at 5,000, 10,000, and 15,000 miles, respectively, are $455, $909, and $1,364. Thus, you save $438, $877 or $1,315 at the respective mileages if you switch from a 14-mpg vehicle to a 27.5-mpg vehicle for the indicated mileages.

WHEN WE'LL BUY | We are waiting for the first turbine car, or some other major engine improvement, before we consider buying. You may move before then when you assess your needs. Knowing what you now know about maintaining and upgrading an automobile, especially if you have been doing some of the work yourself, you are likely to make a more rational choice of new car. You are also likely to find that trying to maintain the powertrain of that new car will be both easier and more difficult: easier if you are willing to trust that electronic controls will do the job reliably and durably, more difficult if the electronics fail. Between 1977 and 1980, the number of electronic switches in some cars increased 50,000 or more. It is likely to continue to increase. That poses a double dilemma. We mentioned that if you seek to do things yourself, your options are going to be relearning the car or blind trust. But the other problem is that there are hundreds of thousands of mechanics out there who will be obsolete unless they, too, learn. They must learn or lose business. The usual way for such people to learn is hands-on experience with customers' cars for practice. Will they learn on your car?

Electronics are wonderful. They promise to be the universal Band-Aid of the auto industry. All these switches are extending the life of the conventional engine by making it work as close to perfection as possible. Of course, the conventional engine itself is inherently less efficient than other engine designs.

Still another pitfall as electronics takes over cars is the almost immediate obsolescence of electronics components. An example: the electronic engine controls (EEC) on some 1978 U.S. cars were at least four times larger and much more complex than the successor system on 1980 cars, yet they were less efficient. If you wanted to integrate that into your 1973 pride and joy, at what point in the development are you going to pay to install the EEC system, assuming you can find a technician capable of doing so? Or at what point will you consider the advancement worth buying new—1981, 1983, 1985? Another large question is how the companies that have prospered supplying replacement parts and accessories in competition with original equipment will react. Electronics ups the stakes considerably. We suspect that some companies will be very active in supplying additional electronics components; for instance, there are already any number of electronic ignition systems on the market.

It is a different matter with the computers that are being sold by firms outside the auto makers. These computers are designed as add-ons. They are relatively easy to install and are "watchers" rather than "doers." They monitor the vehicle for certain information; they don't control any part of its operation. Aside from systems that give you trip and fuel-economy information, these computers do not compete with the bulk of car-maker uses. Control of the actual combustion process seems likely to continue to be the bailiwick of the original-equipment manufacturers.

For 1981 car makers began controlling electronically the combustion process to meet emission standards. For 1982 this will be simplified and a form of fuel injection will be used generally. For 1983 more simplification and system integration will occur. Where do you join the new car buyers?

No matter what new car you buy, however, the rules for body and interior maintenance will remain virtually unchanged in the foreseeable future. You will still need rustproofing, even if more reinforced plastic and aluminum components are phased in. You will still need to protect the paint, the carpeting. You will still clean and expend elbow grease. Finally, if you decide to buy a new car, you will face a more difficult choice than ever before. There are fewer and fewer all-purpose vehicles. Every auto company has indicated a desire to increase, not decrease, the number of cars on the road through more special-purpose units. A two-seater sports car is a special-purpose vehicle, as is a two-seat commuter and shopping car—but they obviously would be very different. A four-wheel-drive Eagle shares that feature with a four-wheel-drive Bronco, but they, too, are very different in concept and purpose.

If the car you are making last and last is a six-passenger general-purpose vehicle, you very well may opt to keep it as part of your fleet, because that kind of car may cost an average of $12,000 or more next year or the year after. It may pay you to purchase that specialty commuter-shopper —maybe not in a two-passenger configuration, but in two-plus-two instead. And then make that car last and last, too.

Assume your automobile is giving you perfectly good

service, has what you consider reasonable gas economy, and you like it for other reasons, too. What would or should make you think of selling it for a new car? We can give the answer only from our point of view, but it may provide thinking points for you. We would change if:

- We could get a car in our price range that fits our life style and transportation needs *and* gives us at least twice the fuel economy and range of our present vehicle. We also want *full* four-passenger space, exceptional acceleration, exceptional (by previous U.S. standards) handling and roadholding. Decent styling is taken for granted. No such car exists now for us.

- We could get a vehicle in our price range that at least surpasses our present car in economy and range and also excites us for its safety, quality of construction, and ability to go in any weather. No such car exists now for us.

- We could get a vehicle in our price range that surpasses our present vehicle's safety and other mentioned qualities and also really is built to last and last and last with minimum maintenance. That car, too, does not exist yet. It will take some kind of breakthrough in corporate thinking to make such vehicles come true.

DREAMS AND ILLUSIONS

Perhaps we all will wake up some fine day and find that someone has found a way to convert all the cars in America to run on hydrogen or some direct derivation thereof. The technology is available at this minute, but the fuel in an economic and safe form is not, except in test amounts, at this writing.

Maybe the millennium will arrive and America will not remain in bondage to the past and will promote some fuel that does not need to be imported. But don't count on it as a national policy. Oil, which we should be utilizing increasingly to make the chemicals that we turn into plastics, insulation, fabrics, and even comestibles, will continue to be wasted on running cars, trucks, and industry.

This land of falling expectations and constricting life styles, which we call America, does not have to lose another freedom, but it is happening nevertheless. Daily we lose our mobility. There is only one hope. America is entering a time again when it will be up to the individual to cope to live. We see it in the return to wood heat and the proliferation of home gardens. Maybe the solutions in transport are all individual—an ethanol converter in every backyard and a photovoltaic cell bank on every roof. Maybe then we can refurbish the American Dream before it becomes a memory.

A Simple Guide to How Your Car Works

The fact that your automobile is a complex piece of machinery need not awe you. You don't have to be a mechanical engineer to learn how to use that complex piece of machinery to perform its primary function—getting people from point A to point B. But you do need to know how a car works in general and in particular. In general means knowing what each component system is generally supposed to do in relation to the other parts. In particular means knowing how your specific automobile works in detail. Your owner's manual will give you the particulars. The general background will follow here.

Why do you need to know? Because if you don't know, you are at the mercy of every person who claims to know. You have no way of judging whether repair work has helped you or ripped you off. You also have no way of judging if a new car really has worthwhile improvements, or whether any component or option is worth the money. You are a blind person trying to read an eye chart in a school for the deaf.

Stand back and look at your car. It is essentially a rectangular shape with a wheel at each corner just like the kind of wagon that horses and men pulled centuries ago. The difference is that a motor and a drivetrain make the wheels turn, not a horse or a man. There is a sophisticated suspension and wheel system to make the ride safer and more comfortable at speed. And it has a steering wheel, not a tiller or reins.

The Motor and Drivetrain   For the foreseeable future, the motor is likely to be an internal-combustion piston type.

That means inside the engine a mixture of gasoline and air is being exploded (burned) in order to force the pistons connected to a crankshaft to move up and down. Each piston is housed in a separate cylinder, and the explosion that forces it to move is so timed that as it goes up, the turning crank forces other pistons partially or fully down, evacuating the leftover gases at the same time. Unless you make model engines for a hobby, you will never see this process.

Most engines are the type where the air and fuel are mixed before they enter the combustion chamber. Their true name is an Otto cycle, something you never may refer to again.

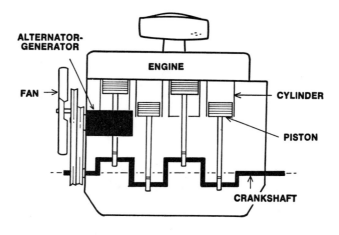

All you really need to know about this part of the process is that a conventional automobile engine in good condition will emit a steady throbbing sound. The more cylinders it has, the smoother the throbbing sound will be. Most cars have either, 4, 6, or 8, although a few have 12—and there are both 16- and 32-cylinder exotic creations still around. When you hear a break in that throb—it's time to see your resident mechanical genius.

A diesel engine also has pistons going up and down, but it works by compressing a measured amount of air until it heats to a temperature sufficient to ignite the fuel injected at that precise moment. This permits it to burn oil instead of gasoline. It gets better fuel economy because it operates at a higher temperature, burning the fuel more completely. But because of the pressure involved, diesel engines are usually heavier. They never have carburetors and they make a clattering noise when they idle. The only other production auto engine is found exclusively in some Mazdas at this writing. It is called a Wankel or rotary engine. It substitutes two triangular rotors for the pistons and cylinders. These form combustion chambers as they rotate in a housing shaped like an ellipse that has been compressed slightly in the middle. Rotary motion has none of the vibrations of piston types, so it is smooth and quiet.

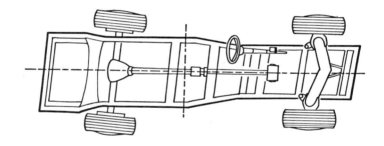

FRAME OUT OF ALIGNMENT

But nowadays you might want to know a bit more than just about engines.

An automobile is a mechanism made up of a frame and body, the powertrain, the steering suspension and wheels, and accessories. We'll skip the accessories and dismiss the frame and the body, assuming you don't let it rust and you aren't involved in a crash. The latter is most important, because if your car frame is bent out of alignment even a little, it could affect handling. That's why you should have an expert check frame alignment, especially after what you might consider a minor accident.

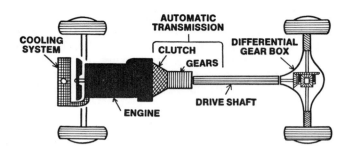

Powertrain Is Motion   The powertrain, like almost every part of the car, does what the name says—it makes the car move. It is composed of the engine and the drivetrain, including the transmission, the ring and pinion gears, and the differential and various shafts.

The powertrain is the most complicated part of the car. Open the hood of your car to look at the engine. It's that large assembly dominating most of the space. If it is a conventional piston engine, the largest part is the engine block; bolted on top of it is the head and intake manifold, and usually on top of that (under the air filter) is the carburetor. The fan, radiator, and battery are immediately recognizable, but if this is an average American car, you may not be able to see underneath the block where the crankcase and exhaust manifold are. Nor the transmission.

The hollow cylinders are inside the engine block. The pistons move up and down inside them, turning the crankshaft. Either on top of each cylinder, or on the side, there are intake and exhaust valves and a spark plug. In most makes on the road today, the sequence of opening and closing is done in a cycle of four strokes—hence, four-cycle engine.

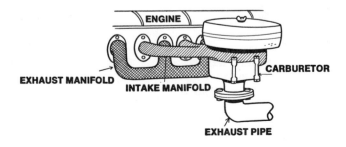

INTAKE COMPRESSION EXPLOSION EXHAUST

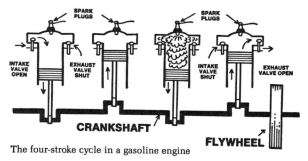

The four-stroke cycle in a gasoline engine

1) The intake valve opens as the piston moves down, admitting the fuel mixture.

2) Both intake and exhaust valves close for the compression stroke as the piston moves up.

3) The particular spark plug emits a spark, igniting the compressed fuel mixture, which expands as it burns. This pushes the piston down.

4) As the exhaust valve opens, the piston rises and pushes out the gases created in the burning.

Comparison of rotary engine with American V-8 developing about the same brake horsepower

There are also two-cycle engines, which combine these functions into two strokes, and, as mentioned, diesel cycle and Wankels.

161

Fuel Becomes Energy Let's follow the gas from the tank to where it becomes mechanical energy. This is the quickest way to see how everything ties together and why the piston four-cycle engine is ultimately doomed to disappear.

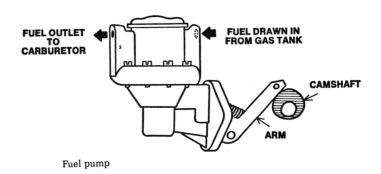

Fuel pump

The fuel pump pumps fuel from the tank through lines to the carburetor. The pump either pulls the gas up or, in some of the latest models, it pushes the fuel up; auto makers are introducing a sealed electric pump into the gas tank to do the pushing. This eliminates problems like vapor lock and pretty much defeats frozen fuel lines unless you are floating on an iceberg in the Bering Sea or buying cheap fuel diluted with water.

The fuel has now arrived at the carburetor, a device to change the liquid gasoline, which will *not* burn explosively, into an atomized air-filled mixture that will. The carburetor is either atop the engine or hanging on the side. The mixture falls (gravity feed) or is forced (forced draft) into the intake manifold, which is a passageway into the various cylinders. The carburetor is controlled by the accelerator pedal. When you "step on the gas," you open valves within the carburetor to force a richer fuel mixture.

We should mention fuel injection here, because this is an alternative, more precise, and more expensive way of doing what the carburetor does. The precision of fuel amounts injected via this system promotes more complete combustion. And soon you may have carburetors that are computer-controlled, which will release precise amounts of fuel and air into the intake manifold.

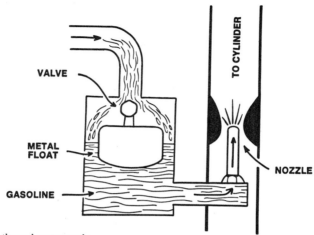

VALVE

TO CYLINDER

METAL
FLOAT

NOZZLE

GASOLINE

How the carburetor works

Inside the Engine   Let's pick up on the gasoline, which has now been harnessed and changed into motion or power turning the heart of the engine—the crankshaft. The crankshaft looks like a steel bar that was caught in a waffle iron. It changes the up-and-down motion of the pistons into rotary motion. It turns the fan and the alternator-generator via a belt. And it also pumps the cooling-system liquid through the walls of the cylinder block and around the outsides of the cylinders to and from the radiator.

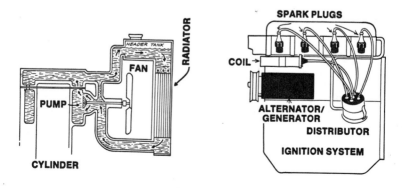

HEADER TANK

RADIATOR

FAN

PUMP

CYLINDER

SPARK PLUGS

COIL

ALTERNATOR/
GENERATOR

DISTRIBUTOR

IGNITION SYSTEM

How the cooling system works

This cooling keeps the engine from burning itself up. The crankshaft itself and the lower parts of the cylinders are cooled and lubricated also by a constant bath of oil housed in the crankcase. That's why oil and radiator liquid must be regularly topped off—unless you appreciate having an engine that may someday cough on some deserted road like an antitobacco commercial and grind to a heated halt.

Back to the generator or alternator, which generates electrical current, which in turn is intensified by the coil. This current is then sent to the distributor (that's the part with the spark plug wires coming out of its head), which in turn distributes the current in sequence to the spark plugs. As for the electricity to start the engine, that comes from the battery. You turn the key in the ignition and this permits battery current to crank the starter motor, which initially fires the engine. Once the engine is turned over and starts, the battery's power ideally will be replaced for its next task.

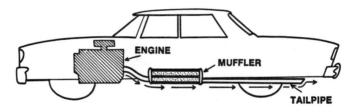

How the exhaust system works

The part of the fuel mixture that did not burn used to be expelled through the exhaust pipe via the exhaust manifold, with the noise pollution abated thanks to the car's muffler. These exhaust gases are now likely to be recirculated into the engine for more complete combustion. Catalytic mufflers—extra mufflers that contain a material to change exhaust gases chemically—are the antipollution order of the day, despite some worries over the heat they exude and the resultant chemical (a member of the sulfide family).

Drive On   Now about the drivetrain. It is the connection that transmits the motion created by the motor to the wheels that drive the car. On a front-wheel-drive car it drives the front

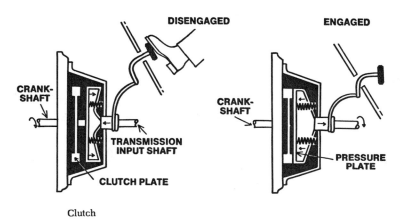

Clutch

wheels. On a rear-drive car it drives the rear wheels. On a four-wheel drive it drives all wheels. When the engine is in the front and the wheels to be driven in the rear, there is a long shaft under the car. When both engine and driving wheels are either in the front or rear, the drivetrain is very compact and more complicated.

Attached to one end of the crankshaft is a device called a clutch. A clutch is two disks facing one another, one of them on the crankshaft and the other on the gearbox. These two clutch plates are held together by springs. Ordinarily when one plate turns, so does the other. Pushing the clutch pedal in a car with a manual shift disengages the clutch plates, thus disconnecting the engine from the driving wheels. This allows the gearbox to be utilized, shifting from one gear to another.

Why do you need a gearbox? It's very logical—because engine power must be transferred in such a way that the driving wheels need not turn at the same speed as the engine. Obviously, for heavy pulling or climbing hills, the engine must turn more rapidly, yet the wheels may move slowly. At turnpike speeds, there is little loading on the engine and it is desirable to select the highest gear.

The gearbox of a standard (manual) transmission consists of a series of interconnecting toothed disks of different sizes called gears. If you have a three-speed transmission, you have three forward gears plus a reverse gear; if you have a four-speed transmission, you have four forward gears plus a reverse. You control the gears with a gear shift.

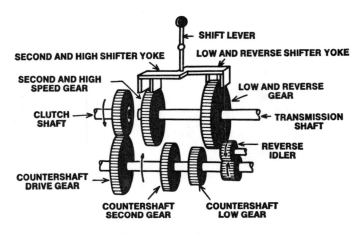

Transmission with gears in neutral

An automatic transmission, American style, replaces the clutch and sometimes all the gears with a liquid coupling system slightly less efficient in controlling power but much more convenient. This also eliminates the clutch pedal. In a manual/automatic, more common on imported cars, there can be conventional gears, but the shifting is done either mechanically, electromagnetically, or in an oil bath.

The gear (or driving range) selected determines how fast the drive shaft turns. The drive shaft connects the transmission to the rear axle, to which the driving wheels are attached. But the power is coming in at right angles to this rear axle, so its direction must be changed again. This is the job of the ring and pinion gears. The pinion gear on the drive shaft drives the ring gear, thus accomplishing the direction change.

We have one other set of gears to traverse before the power turns a wheel—the differential. (Look under the car. The differential is in that bell-shaped housing on the rear axle.) It compensates for the fact that on turns and curves, the inner wheels travel a shorter distance than the outer wheels. Ever watch a chorus line in an ice show do a pinwheel routine? As the whirling line gets longer, the skaters on the outside must skate faster and faster to keep up with those in the middle, who are hardly moving. The differential gears let relative wheel speed govern which way the power is

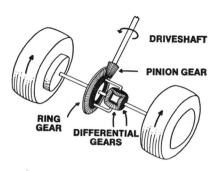

DRIVESHAFT

PINION GEAR

RING
GEAR

DIFFERENTIAL
GEARS

Conventional differential

supplied. A limited-slip differential is a special version, which limits slippage between differential gears so that the wheel with the most traction gets the greatest power supply. This is valuable in most driving situations involving either a wet road or sand and mud.

Now you know generally how the most complicated part of the car works. There will still be people who will try to one-up you by talking about viscous-drive fans (a fan that disconnects itself after the vehicle reaches a certain steady speed) or some other less common detail. So get your own pet mechanism.

Steering Systems Let's talk about the "forgotten" part of the car—that is, the steering and suspension systems, including the wheels and tires. If you care to notice, tires are the only parts of the car that actually contact the road. In other words, the whole complicated powertrain is there only to make the tires roll. But cars wouldn't be very popular if you could only get them to go in a straight line. Thus the driver must be able to *steer* the machine.

That brings us to a round shape inside the car that's too prominent to ignore—the steering wheel; it seems attached to a column and it turns. The wheel really is connected to a shaft inside the steering column; the shaft in turn is connected to the turning wheels of the car via one of several types of shaft-and-gear arrangement.

Worm-and-roller is common: this means there is a worm gear, which turns a roller, which in turn makes the turning wheels point in the direction you want. You *did* notice that (assuming you are going forward) the car goes to the right if you turn the steering wheel to the right—that's getting down to the real basics, isn't it?

Another common system is rack-and-pinion: here a pinion gear controls an arrangement of shafts shaped like a rack to do the turning. Like other systems, it is constructed to help stop most road-shock feedback but not all. You have to have some "feel" of the road surface and adjust your driving accordingly. Thus the steering also functions as part of the suspension.

There is one other fact you should know: steering shafts are segmented as a safety measure for all cars in the U.S. market; that makes it more difficult for them to act as spears to shish-kebab you if your car crashes.

Suspension Systems   Other major components of the suspension are the wheels and tires, the shock absorbers, and the springs. Springs have been around in one form or another since prehistory. Man soon found out that a chariot or a wagon without springs made riding uncomfortable if not impossible. The leather thongs and crude metal devices of yesterday have given way to the modern spring, highly sophisticated not so much in shape as in the utilization of the physical properties of the material used.

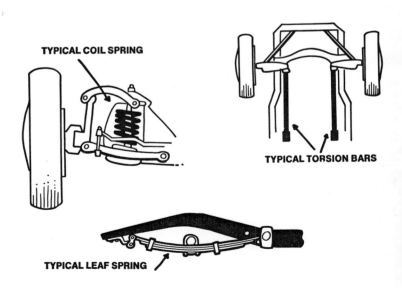

TYPICAL COIL SPRING

TYPICAL TORSION BARS

TYPICAL LEAF SPRING

There are three kinds of modern spring configuration used in the auto suspension—leaf springs, coil springs, and torsion bars. All springs rely on the inherent property of metal—in most cases spring steel—to seek its original shape. (Steel is more elastic than rubber.) Other materials and systems have been and are being used—one company has an air-oil system encased in rubber, another system based on the compression properties of liquids. Fiberglass and other composites have been the subject of experiments. But at present most car suspensions employ steel. The 1981 Corvette is the current exception with a rear leaf spring.

All kinds of steel springs have one thing in common. They place the metal device under tension, controlling its rate of rebound. This is called the device's spring rate. More than any other factor, the spring rate determines whether the suspension is still or soft. If you feel one or two jolts and that's it when you hit a bump, the suspension is stiff. If you feel or hear a succession of small bumps or vibrations, it's soft.

Coil springs illustrate how this is done. The lower coils of the spring are thicker and can be slightly larger in diameter of coil than the upper coils. Leaf springs are strips of steel with interliners: the number of leaves, their shape, and the nature of the steel all control how stiff a suspension they give.

Torsion bars look the simplest yet are the most sophisticated metal spring on cars. They are rods of steel—either one-piece or laminated—twisted so they are under torsional tension and then attached. They react with exceptional sensitivity to the road surface and, in addition, because they twist instead of bounce, they eliminate much of the rebound that is a design factor in coils and leaves. But we are told they are a bit more expensive as a system and thus have not captured the spring market. Chrysler Corporation, however, employs them extensively.

Springs hardly ever break, but their shackles and attachment hardware sometimes do. If your car suddenly seems to ride very hard and you have checked for a flat or for an unbalanced wheel, get your springs checked while the car is up on a rack. Sometimes replacing a mounting or a shackle can restore ride quality.

Springs absorb road shock and distribute it in the car frame and body. The shock absorbers further refine this road shock and also help counteract what you would likely call sway when the car makes a turn. If you remember your jack-in-the-box, the head swayed from side to side after the coil spring underneath popped him out. That pitching motion is what the shock must control. If it does not—in other words if you have worn shock absorbers—the car will pitch on turns, making it hard to control. Now you have still another component (there are four shocks) to check, especially if you think ride quality has deteriorated.

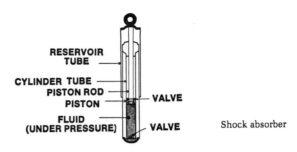

RESERVOIR TUBE

CYLINDER TUBE
PISTON ROD
PISTON — VALVE

FLUID
(UNDER PRESSURE) — VALVE

Shock absorber

The most common shock absorber in a modern car is made so that the piston inside it moves up and down, as the road surface dictates, pushing against oil or trapped air or an inert gas like nitrogen. You can make a rough check yourself of the shocks and the springs by pushing down on any extreme corner of the car. If you feel no resistance or if the end continues to rebound after you let go, have an expert examine the shocks.

Tire-Wheel Combinations   We come now to the only part of the car that contacts the road—the tire and wheel combination. They should be thought of as a unit, because each is useless without the other. Yet choice of either tire or wheel can affect the handling and safety of the car faster and more directly than any other part. Most auto wheels that come as stock equipment on modern cars are made of pressed steel; they are not perfectly round, although you can't tell that with the naked eye. Stock passenger-car tires, even when inflated properly, also are not perfectly round.

A perfectly round tire-wheel would roll more easily, hold direction more truly, and even stop more accurately. From this description you can infer that the idea of the tire-wheel combination is to use the car's power to roll in the indicated direction as efficiently as possible. In other words, the less rolling resistance when the car is supposed to be moving, the better.

There is no such thing as a perfectly round tire-wheel combination. However, the closer you can approach this, the better. Generally certain types of premium tires (such as the Pirelli P6), because they are made more carefully, approach this ideal and stay closer to it during their life because of their construction.

Rolling resistance is a factor of not only the roundness of the tire-wheel but also its weight as compared to the other tires on the car, particularly its opposite member. That is one reason why wheels are balanced; the other is to ensure better directional stability. Ideally every tire-wheel combination should be balanced against every other on the car. Then you can switch them around. You are playing the fool if you do not have your tires balanced.

Wheeling It   There are wheels and there are wheels. It depends on whether you are prepared to spend extra money for certain benefits. Most of it has to do with reducing the unsprung weight on cars with conventional suspensions to get better ride quality. It is desirable to have wheels that are lighter than the production version also, because the lighter the total car, the better power-to-weight ratio there is. In other words, you can run faster and longer on the same amount of stamina carrying a 10-pound package than if you are carrying a 40-pound package.

Magnesium wheels are the lightest, but they may not be worth it to you because you must use tubes within your tires; that metal is porous enough to let air escape. There are combination aluminum-and-steel wheels, cast-aluminum wheels, and lightweight steel wheels. If they are properly engineered, they can help and they also look great. There are also wire wheels with wire spokes extending like radii from the wheel hub. Besides being light, these wheels may absorb more road shock than other types, and they are much sought after by sports-car purists. If you are going to replace wheels, you must remember to get the correct size, both for your car and the tire you want to use. (Soon there may be wheels of reinforced plastic, too.)

Tires on the modern car must be inflated with air under pressure. That's all you need to know and remember, once you have made the selection of what kind of tire is best for the amount and type of driving you do. No matter what kind you choose, they must be kept at proper air pressures for maximum comfort, safety and durability.

Braking Systems   We purposely have put off talking about stopping the car until we had covered tires, because they are such an important component of the process. Since they are the part that contacts the road, the nature of their reaction when you hit the brake pedal is at least as important as the kind of braking system you have.

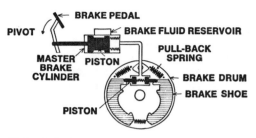

Hydraulic braking system

Let's start from the brake pedal. When you press down with your foot on this pedal, you are pushing against brake fluid in the master cylinder, which in turn distributes that pressure via fluid in the brake lines to the actual brakes on each wheel. If you have drum brakes, the brake shoes are forced against the brake drums attached to the wheel. If you have disk brakes, calipers with pads are squeezed against a plate attached to the wheel. In either case, friction is used to stop, and there is a wearing process in which heat is created. The brake fluid absorbs some of this heat and is formulated to accept it. Disk brakes are more efficient but generate more heat and need special brake fluid. They also do not react kindly to people who drive with one foot resting on the brake pedal, since they are so sensitive. This brings the pads into contact with the plate and wears them unnecessarily. Keep your foot off the brake pedal unless you are slowing or stopping.

The parking brake is a separate mechanical brake that either locks the hydraulic brakes or has a separate brake within a brake to do that. It is also an emergency brake to stop abruptly if the hydraulic system fails.

When the wheel is slowed, the tire is also forced to stop rolling and more friction and heat are generated. The tread of the tire is rubbed against the road surface, aiding the slowing process. Ideally that tread will not squirm, and the sipes and ridges in it will remain open to take care of water on the road, to help dissipate heat, and to retain directional control for the driver. Whether the tread will function properly is the result of many factors, not the least of which is the tire construction.

Tire Types   The single easiest way to transform the performance of any car is to put better tires on it. Many times it's the best move toward safety. And the best time to make the switch is when you get your new car. Use the best tires you can afford, and never use racing or agricultural tires on a passenger car.

There are literally thousands of variations in tires, a fact you should dismiss immediately unless you are going into the business. They all fall into general types and price categories. The types now available are the bias ply, the bias belted, and the radial ply tire or belted radial.

**RADIAL PLY
PREMIUM**

**BIAS BELTED
AVERAGE PRICE**

**BIAS PLY
(CONVENTIONAL)
LOW PRICE**

The bias ply—a ply is one wrapping of tire cord, and most tires on U.S. cars have four or the equivalent—has its cord body, which supports the rubber tread and sidewalls, wrapped in a bias or diagonally. It requires a stiff sidewall to support the tread, but it can be a good, comfortable, and inexpensive-to-make tire.

The bias-belted tire adds a belt or belts going in the same direction as the tread of the tire. This belt of cord acts to firm up the tread, keeping it open for better road contact. It can be a satisfactory tire for U.S. cars.

The radial tire has taken over because it promotes better gas mileage. Its original adoption in the United States, however, was the result of the growing knowledge of its high-performance handling by the American driver. The ability to brake, to accelerate, and to maneuver instantly and still maintain complete car control are characteristic of radial tires.

The radial tire has a light carcass in which cords are perpendicular to the belt; in other words, they extend like radii from the center of the wheel. They are constructed to flex easily, which is why properly inflated radial tires sometimes look flat. The belts, however, are stiff and may be made of steel or fabric cord. These belts hold the tread firm for better stopping and for better rolling. And the radial tire is likely to be rounder, too. Steel-belted radials seem to be the best for durability and extended road mileage and now have totally overcome ride harshness.

It is best not to mix different types of tires, but if you must, put the radials on the rear wheels of a car. In fact, if you have different types of radials, put the fabric on the rear. Belted tires should be bought in sets and balanced that way to get full performance benefits.

Tend to Your Tires   Your personal safety depends on how much attention you give to your car's tires. After all, they are a car's only contact with the road.

Check and adjust tire pressure when the tire is *cold*, either before using your car or several hours after driving it. Use a pressure gauge *regularly*—a difference of 2 to 4 psi (pounds per square inch) can affect tire performance and tread wear.

If you ride on bias-ply, bias-belted, or most radial tires, rotate the tires every 6,000 miles to even out tread wear. One exception is the steel-belted radial. It never has to be rotated if your car is kept in reasonably good shape, tires are properly inflated, and wheels balanced.

Underinflation causes extreme tire flexing and builds up excessive heat, running the risk of blowout. It also causes rapid wear on the outer edges of the tread and reduces road-holding ability.

Overinflation causes tires to run hard and subjects them to impact damages and weakening of the carcass. It also causes excessive wear in the center of the tread and reduces cornering power.

Proper inflation with the pressure (psi) recommended by the manufacturer for full contact of the tire with the road.

Improper wheel balance on any car can cause a "shimmy" and "wobble" that affects steering. If a tire and wheel have one extra-heavy area, they will slam the road continuously and result in a flat spot on the tire tread.

If one side of the tread on either front wheel is wearing more rapidly than the rest, check your front-end alignment. It doesn't take much—a pothole or two—to knock a car's wheels out of line.

There are danger signals—signs of tread wear—that you must look for on a regular basis. Any disappearance of tread pattern or design will result in loss of traction. When bars of solid rubber called "wear indicators" appear all the way across the tread, the tire is worn out and should be thrown away.

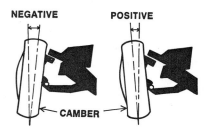

Wheel alignment

Snow Tires Not for Summer Snow tires are not as wear-resistant as standard highway tires in summer. The heavier snow tire runs "hotter" on dry pavements and wears faster. Also, your chances of experiencing tire damage, owing to heat buildup, are increased as external temperatures rise. There are new "stickier" snow tires on the market with a still softer rubber compound and fiberglass belts. They are said to ride quieter than conventional snow tires but they should also be removed for spring.

A bumpier ride and road noise should be reason enough for putting snow tires in cold storage. Don't be a summer snow-tire holdout! The tire change will save you tread wear and money.

Drive Smoothly If you have paid attention, you now should know just about everything necessary about the car and its parts. The hard part remains: knowing about the final component —you, the driver. There are millions of drivers around the world who think they know how to drive and have licenses from the state to prove it. These millions would benefit tremendously from an elementary course in the subject.

Since this is unlikely, you must drive to protect yourself. You must make sure you are alert at all times to what the car beyond the car in front of you will do—and the car behind the car in back of you—and the traffic and people on your flanks. You must give adequate warning when you are going to turn and you must use caution when passing.

The basic, and most important, smooth driving technique is driving ahead of your car. A 12-second visual search pattern is recommended to give you time to scan the road ahead and anticipate trouble before it happens. In other words you must be viewing the road for what you will need to do in 12 seconds. For example, a smooth stop is made by the driver who sees the traffic light, or any other reason for stopping, far ahead of time. The driver who simply rushes the light is gambling his life on the chance that it may change before he crosses the intersection.

When you are turning, try to use all the road available to you. Making a *large* curve is easier to maintain, easier also on your tires, your brakes, and more critically on your safety. To make a "smooth turn," slow down and lightly brake before getting into the curve. When you are halfway through the curve, accelerate with moderation. The added speed will help you gain control and ensure a smooth return to the straightaway.

Another technique to practice is to avoid using the brakes as much as possible. Brakes, as you know, work by slowing or stopping the wheels, *not* the car itself. This means they create extra friction between the tires and the road. Old tires may blow out from too much heat too soon, and smooth tires—those with worn-out treads—may often cause skidding.

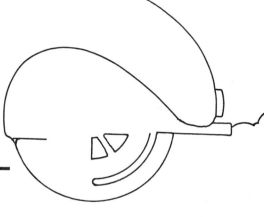

Appendix Two

How Much Do You Pay for Gas Each Year?

5,000 MILES

Miles per Gallon	Price per Gallon							
	$1.00	**$1.15**	**$1.25**	**$1.50**	**$1.75**	**$2.00**	**$2.25**	**$2.50**
12	$417	$479	$521	$625	$729	$833	$937	$1041
14	357	411	446	536	625	714	804	893
16	312	359	391	469	547	625	703	781
18	278	319	347	417	486	556	625	694
20	250	287	312	375	437	500	562	625
22	227	261	284	341	398	455	511	568
24	208	240	260	312	365	417	469	521
26	192	221	240	288	337	385	433	481
27.5	**182**	**209**	**227**	**273**	**318**	**364**	**409**	**455**
28	179	205	223	268	312	357	402	446
30	167	192	208	250	292	333	375	417
32	156	180	195	234	273	312	352	391
34	147	169	184	221	257	294	331	368
36	139	160	174	208	243	278	312	347

Miles per Gallon	Price per Gallon							
	$1.00	$1.15	$1.25	$1.50	$1.75	$2.00	$2.25	$2.50
38	132	151	165	198	230	263	296	329
40	125	144	156	187	219	250	281	312
42	119	137	149	179	208	238	268	298
44	114	131	142	170	199	228	256	284
46	109	125	136	163	190	218	245	272
48	104	120	130	156	182	208	234	260
50	100	115	125	150	175	200	225	250

7,500 MILES

Miles per Gallon	Price per Gallon							
	$1.00	$1.15	$1.25	$1.50	$1.75	$2.00	$2.25	$2.50
12	625	719	782	938	1094	1250	1406	1563
14	532	616	670	804	937	1071	1205	1339
16	469	539	586	703	820	938	1055	1172
18	417	479	523	625	729	833	938	1042
20	375	431	469	563	656	750	844	938
22	341	392	426	511	597	682	767	852
24	313	359	391	469	547	625	703	781
26	288	332	361	433	505	577	649	721
27.5	**273**	**314**	**341**	**409**	**477**	**545**	**614**	**682**
28	268	308	335	402	469	536	603	670
30	250	287	313	375	438	500	563	625
32	234	270	338	352	410	469	527	586
34	221	254	276	331	386	441	496	551
36	208	240	260	312	365	417	469	521
38	197	227	247	296	345	395	444	494
40	188	216	234	281	328	375	422	469
42	179	205	223	268	312	357	402	446
44	170	196	213	256	298	341	384	426
46	163	188	204	245	285	326	367	408
48	156	180	195	234	273	312	352	391
50	150	172	187	225	262	300	337	375

10,000 MILES

**Miles
per
Gallon**   **Price per Gallon**

	$1.00	$1.15	$1.25	$1.50	$1.75	$2.00	$2.25	$2.50
12	834	958	1042	1250	1458	1666	1874	2082
14	714	822	892	1072	1250	1428	1608	1786
16	624	718	782	938	1094	1250	1406	1562
18	556	638	694	834	972	1112	1250	1388
20	500	574	624	750	874	1000	1124	1250
22	454	522	568	682	796	910	1022	1136
24	416	480	520	624	730	834	938	1042
26	384	442	480	576	674	770	866	962
27.5	**364**	**418**	**455**	**545**	**636**	**727**	**818**	**909**
28	358	410	446	536	624	714	804	892
30	334	384	416	500	584	666	750	834
32	312	360	390	468	566	624	704	782
34	294	338	368	442	514	588	662	736
36	278	320	348	416	486	556	624	694
38	264	302	330	396	460	526	592	658
40	250	288	312	374	438	500	562	624
42	238	274	298	355	416	476	536	596
44	228	262	284	340	398	456	512	568
46	218	250	272	326	380	436	490	544
48	208	240	260	312	364	416	468	520
50	200	230	250	300	350	400	450	500

It is obvious that improving a vehicle from 12 miles per gallon to 14 saves more dollars than improving from 30 mpg to 40. Thus, there is a law of diminishing financial return on improving fuel economy. That doesn't mean you shouldn't strive for the best mpg possible. It does mean that you should assess the cost to achieve the better mileage before upgrading. If there are other factors involved, like performance or antipollution improvements, then you must judge the worth to you.

It is patently obvious, however, that those in the 12-to-20-mpg range have a wide financial incentive to upgrade fuel economy.

Appendix Three

How Much Do You Pay for Financing?

For the purpose of answering the question above, we are not interested in how you obtain the best value for your interest dollar. Obviously, you should shop for financing when you need it and you are entitled to have finance charges explained to you in terms of true annual percentage rather than quoted rates or monthly payments.

Banks, your car dealer, credit unions, and finance companies are all lending you money against the collateral of the new car. Some hedge their bets by insisting you buy life insurance on the loan, or even life insurance plus accident and health insurance. In some states, however, it is illegal to demand that you buy insurance. On very expensive cars you may even pledge other objects of value to get the loan.

There are stratagems to pay the least for the money you need. You can take a loan against your life-insurance policy or one against passbook savings. But you are still paying, no matter what the interest rate. This is money in your pocket if you skip the trade-in cycle.

Following is a table that shows the dollar amounts you would pay for various sizes of auto loans for different time periods, adding the monthly payment.

This is a complex subject and you ought to see your local banker to learn all the nuances. For instance, three years on a 14 percent annual percentage rate for $6,000 finds you paying almost 23 percent of the loan amount in interest.

When people finance an automobile, they may already be juggling various other finance payments—for instance, the credit card purchases, a stereo, a washer. It is very important to give priority to the bill charging the highest rate of interest and pay less on the others in the order of their respective interest charges.

For example, if you can spare $200 from your paycheck for all four items you wish to buy or have bought, here is a comparison.

	Current	**Better**
Stereo (12 percent)	$15	$30
Washer (8 percent)	$15	$50
Credit Card (18 percent)	$30	$60
Available for Car	$95	$140
(8 percent)	$105	$60
	$200	$200

With this strategy in mind, the effective interest rate thus becomes quite important in deciding whether you wish to assume the burden of a new car. Because if you have a limited income for installments, you may need to sacrifice other purchases to the car.

There are a vast variety of loans available, but these are a few basic questions you can ask any banker that will give you all the information you need to make an informed decision.

1. What is the effective (true) annual interest rate?

2. What are the options for longer and shorter terms of repayment?

3. What is the penalty for prepayment?

4. What is the penalty for late payment?

5. Is repayment insurance included? (This is, for instance, in the event that the person buying the car dies in the middle of payments are the survivors liable for keeping up the payments, even though they may be getting rid of the car?)

Index